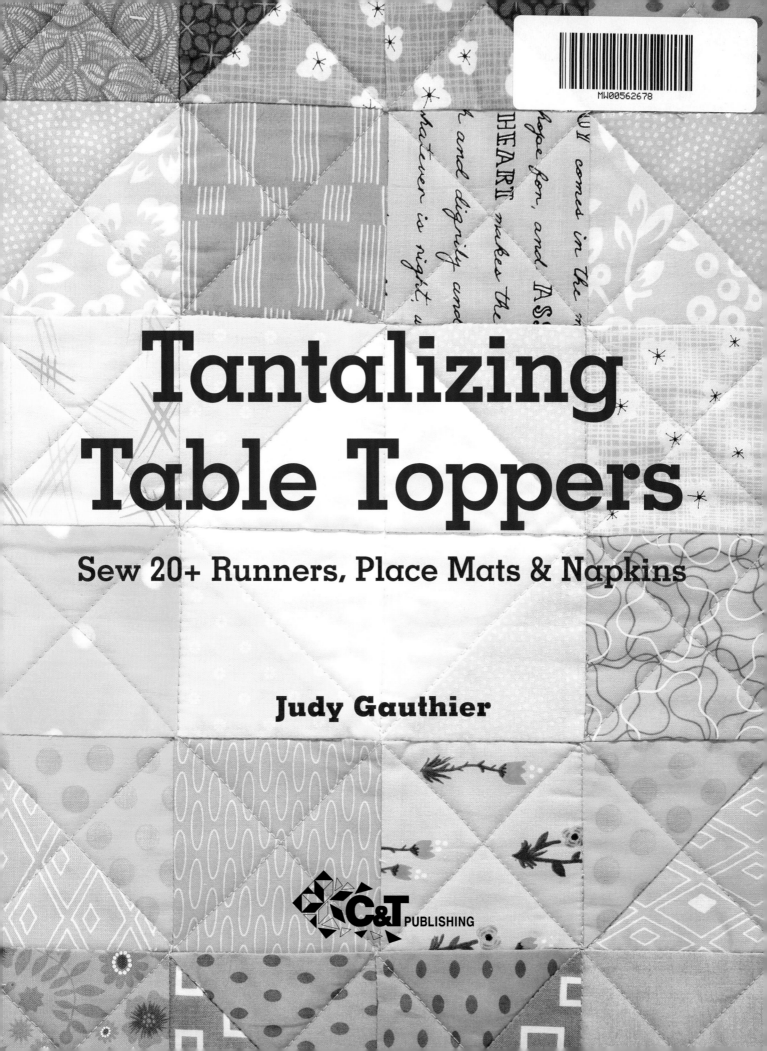

Tantalizing Table Toppers

Sew 20+ Runners, Place Mats & Napkins

Judy Gauthier

C&T PUBLISHING

Text copyright © 2019 by Judy Gauthier

Photography and artwork copyright © 2019 by C&T Publishing, Inc.

PUBLISHER: Amy Marson

CREATIVE DIRECTOR: Gailen Runge

ACQUISITIONS EDITOR: Roxane Cerda

MANAGING EDITOR: Liz Aneloski

EDITOR: Kathryn Patterson

TECHNICAL EDITOR: Debbie Rodgers

COVER/BOOK DESIGNER: April Mostek

PRODUCTION COORDINATOR: Zinnia Heinzmann

PRODUCTION EDITOR: Jennifer Warren

ILLUSTRATOR: Aliza Shalit

PHOTO ASSISTANT: Rachel Holmes

PHOTOGRAPHY by Kelly Burgoyne of C&T Publishing, Inc.

Published by C&T Publishing, Inc., P.O. Box 1456, Lafayette, CA 94549

Library of Congress Cataloging-in-Publication Data

Names: Gauthier, Judy, 1962-

Title: Tantalizing table toppers : sew 20+ runners, place mats & napkins / Judy Gauthier.

Description: Lafayette, CA : C&T Publishing, Inc., [2019]

Identifiers: LCCN 2019002153 | ISBN 9781617458668 (soft cover)

Subjects: LCSH: Patchwork quilts. | Patchwork--Patterns. | Quilting--Patterns. | Table setting and decoration.

Classification: LCC TT835 .G3318 2019 | DDC 746.46/041--dc23

LC record available at https://lccn.loc.gov/2019002153

Printed in China

10 9 8 7 6 5 4 3 2 1

Dedication

To my mother, who always set a beautiful table.
We always used cloth napkins at every meal,
and she would have a lovely tablecloth on the
table every day. Because of her, I have a love of
tablescaping. While I am not a very good cook,
I can sure set a beautiful table.

Contents

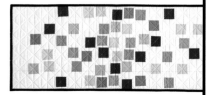

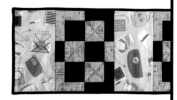

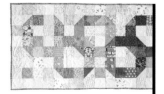

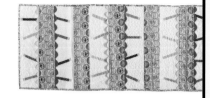
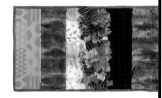
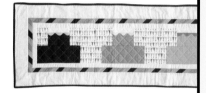
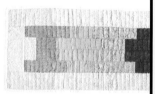

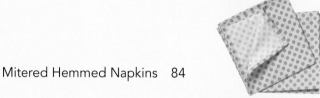

Tablescaping— Setting an Artful Table

Every home has a table, whether in a kitchen or separate dining room. Even in the most remote countries, there is a place for gathering over food, a place for sharing meals. In some areas, I imagine, that place is mainly outside. But for the majority of individuals, couples, and families, the kitchen or dining room table is the heart of the home.

I have always loved to set a beautiful table. It's a dream come true to write a book dedicated to making the dining table an art form. Perhaps this is because I never really prided myself on my cooking skills. Oh, I could cook to get by, but my meals would never win any awards. Don't get me wrong—we all survived in our house. And, just as important, our tables were always impeccably set!

Meal times should be relaxing, and having beautiful table surroundings shouldn't cost much. There are always beautiful dishes, table settings, and utensils for sale at secondhand stores. You can also find pitchers, vases, and serving dishes at resale shops, and these can complete any tablescaping theme. If you are not breaking the bank and are able to set a fabulous table, you'll feel great. Plus, your guests will enjoy everything so much more if they're surrounded by artful settings.

This book contains directions for making twenty different table runners as well as several types of place mats and napkins, any of which can be made to match a table runner just by altering the fabric choices. Have fun with it!

An elaborately tablescaped table. It doesn't have to be this dramatic to have a successful gathering—use your imagination!

General Instructions

There are a few housekeeping items to cover before we set off on our journey of making some really great projects.

Unless otherwise specified, all seam allowances in this book are ¼˝, yardages are based on fabric that measures 44˝ wide, and pieces are stitched with right sides together.

I like to work using basic squares. Most of my designs involve using squares that are 3½˝, 4½˝, or 5½˝; sometimes I use all three in a pattern by combining them in interesting ways. There are certainly projects in this book that don't use these sizes, but many do. If you don't already have templates in these sizes, I would suggest purchasing some. I like to use fast2cut Simple Square Templates (by C&T Publishing). They come all together in a packet, and often-times a 5½˝ template is hard to find!

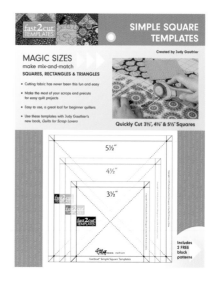

Making Half-Square Triangles

One other design element that you will find repeated in this book is the use of half-square triangles. There are several different ways to make half-square triangles, and I am sure that many people have their favorite ways. The half-square triangles in this book are made as follows.

1. Place 2 squares of fabric right sides together. Usually these are contrasting squares.

2. Using a rigid ruler and a marking pen or pencil, draw a line from corner to opposite corner.

3. Stitch a ¼˝ seam on both sides of the line.

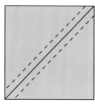

4. Cut along the solid line as drawn. Each pairing of fabrics creates 2 half-square triangle blocks.

5. Open out the half-square triangle blocks and press. Press to the darker of the 2 fabrics. Square the blocks to the size indicated in the pattern.

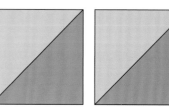

Using Rickrack

Several of the patterns call for rickrack. Rickrack adds a fun and festive look to anything to which it is applied. However, there are some tips that are useful when applying it. Adding rickrack to a piece of fabric causes the fabric to "shrink up." As the rickrack is sewn onto the piece of fabric, the fabric under it tends to gather ever so slightly. You may not even notice it; however, rickrack shortens the fabric it is being sewn to. Because of this, it is often wise to cut the piece of fabric ¼˝–½˝ longer than directed. After the rickrack is sewn to the piece of fabric, measure it again. Square it to the appropriate size.

Rickrack should be sewn to the edge of the fabric with half of the "humps" above the edge of the fabric and half below. You should see a small edge of fabric above the concave line.

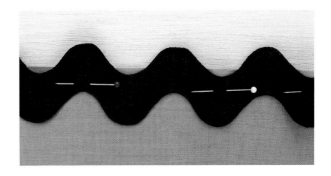

The rickrack should be basted with a longer basting stitch, about ⅛˝ below the concave line.

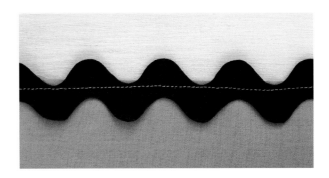

How to Press for Success

Quilters young and old will find in the course of their sewing careers that they change their mind about pressing styles. I am currently in a "press seam allowances open" phase. Prior to this phase, I pressed the seam allowances in the direction that they seemed to want to go. When you have fabrics from different manufacturers or are using fabrics that have different textures in your quilt, the seam allowances will want to lean a particular way. You may end up fighting with them to get them to stay over to one side or another. When you do this, you will find that they will flop back in the direction that they wanted to go anyway; when you sew across them, you will leave a lump or twisted seam allowance.

This seam allowance wants to go where it wants to go!

I always maintain that if you had just left it alone and pressed it in the direction that it desired, you wouldn't have a lump. I still think this is true.

But now—for the most part—I like to press so that my seam allowances nest. Here's an example of nested seam allowances.

Your patchwork intersections will be perfect when you nest them.

When you do it this way, you are butting the seam allowances against each other so that the points of your squares come very close together and are appealing to the eye.

The Theory of Lights, Darks, and Mediums

It seems that every book about quilting has a chapter or section about color intensity, yet it escapes so many of us. *Color intensity* refers to the lightness or darkness of a fabric (in other words, where a fabric falls on the gray scale).

Because I own a quilt shop, I am always involved in helping customers choose the proper fabrics and colors for their projects. Sometimes, the maker selects colors that theoretically go very well together, but for some reason it doesn't scream, "*Wow!*" Oftentimes it's because there isn't enough variation between the lights, darks, and mediums.

Sometimes a customer is trying to make a low-volume quilt and therefore wants all the fabrics to be of one to two intensity levels. But even with a low-volume quilt there are variations between lights and darks.

When you're planning your project and you know which colors you want, it's helpful to have a tool to help you to distinguish between light, dark, and medium. Color intensity is often relative, and you can't always tell from just looking at a fabric if it is light, dark, or medium. It can fool you, and often it does!

For example, look at the piece of fabric below. When you look at it in its original color, it would appear to be a light piece of fabric.

A fabric that appears to be light

But when you look at it with the grayscale setting of a camera, it appears quite a bit darker than you would think. It's closer to a medium than a light.

When the camera is turned to the grayscale setting, the true intensity shows.

Back in the day, we used to have several options for determining the intensity of a fabric. We had ruby beholders and we had black-and-white copiers. But the world of technology has saved us from all that. Simply turn your camera to the grayscale setting and compare your fabrics. It will help you to see which fabrics are light, dark, and medium.

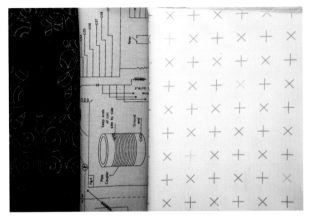

These fabrics have a good range between light, dark, and medium.

Don't get discouraged. It takes practice, just like anything. Remember that beauty is in the eye of the beholder. This is just some information to help the beauty show a little more for the beholder.

The table runner Shattered (page 22) gives you a chance to practice using lights, darks, and mediums, and to make a low-volume project.

A Note on Texture

Incorporate texture in your tablescapes! Texture does wonders for a table. Pull in faux furs and shag furs. Use fabrics that have glitter and glitz, and don't be afraid to use confetti! You will find that several of the projects included here emphasize texture in fabrics and technique (for examples, see The Textured Table, page 59, and The Fabric Makes It, page 67).

Table Runners

A quilt is an item of comfort. But quilts in a kitchen or dining room? Well, they don't naturally work in that environment. So quilters and sewists have done the next best thing: the table runner. It is the perfect intersection between quilting, cooking, and the love that surrounds a family table and a family meal.

The best part about a table runner is that it can instantly change the look of your kitchen and make you happy every time you enter that room. Even if your kitchen is nothing more than a tiny table and a stove, or just a counter, a well-placed table runner can make your heart sing every time it comes into view.

Most of the same quilting principles apply to table runners as they do to quilts. A table runner can be very satisfying because it can be completed in far less time than it takes to make a full quilt. And if you like the blocks in the table runners in this book, the blocks can certainly be reproduced to make a quilt.

I've always found that a table runner is much more satisfying work than a wallhanging. Personally, I don't ever do wallhangings. But a table runner? I will make that in a heartbeat. I always say that in 100 years, if someone finds my table runner or my quilts, they will always know what to do with them. But they may not know what to do with a wallhanging.

To Have and To Hold

Finished table runner: 24½˝ × 63½˝

It seems that people often have large reception tables for a wedding party, and many people now have large farmhouse tables. A small table runner can look dwarfed by a large table. This runner will make an impact at a table for a large gathering.

MATERIALS

Light background fabric: 1⅜ yards *or* an equal amount of assorted light scraps, large enough to yield 22 squares 4½˝ × 4½˝ and 96 squares 3½˝ × 3½˝

Assorted scraps of 7 different colors, each large enough to yield 4 squares 4½˝ × 4½˝ and 7 squares 3½˝ × 3½˝

Binding: ½ yard

Backing: 1½ yards

Batting: 28˝ × 68˝

CUTTING

Light background fabric

- Cut 22 squares 4½˝ × 4½˝.

- Cut 96 squares 3½˝ × 3½˝.

Assorted scraps

From each color:

- Cut 4 squares 4½˝ × 4½˝.

- Cut 7 squares 3½˝ × 3½˝.

Binding

- Cut 5 strips 2½˝ × width of fabric.

Make the Half-Square Triangles

NOTE • There are 3 half-square triangle units in this runner that are a combination of 2 colored fabrics. The remainder of the half-square triangle units uses only one color and a background color. Therefore, it is helpful to have the color sequence planned prior to construction or to use a design wall.

1. Refer to Making Half-Square Triangles (page 8) to make 3 half-square triangle units *each* of the first 6 colors, using 3 background squares 4½″ × 4½″ and 3 colored squares 4½″ × 4½″. Make 4 half-square triangles for color 7. You will have a remaining half-square triangle unit for each combination that won't be used.

2. Using a 4½″ × 4½″ colored square and a 4½″ × 4½″ colored square from the next ring in the runner, make 3 of the combination half-square triangle blocks. Refer to the photo (page 13). You will have a remaining half-square triangle unit for each combination that won't be used.

3. Square all the half-square triangle units and trim to 3½″ × 3½″.

Construct the Columns

1. The runner is constructed in 21 columns, using the first color and then moving into the second color.

2. Stitch together 8 background squares 3½″ × 3½″ in a column. Press the seams in the direction of the arrow.

3. Stitch the second column of squares together. The second and fifth units in the column will be half-square triangle units. Refer to the photo (page 13). Note the orientation of the half-square triangle units.

4. Continue in this manner until all 21 columns have been sewn, using the arrows as a guide for the direction of pressing the seam allowances.

5. Stitch the columns together. Press the seam allowances to either side.

Finishing

Layer the top, batting, and backing. Quilt and bind in the desired manner.

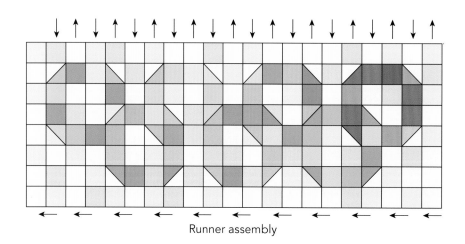

Runner assembly

Color Wave

Finished table runner: 18½˝ × 42½˝

With this table runner, you don't use all the colors of the rainbow—just your favorite ones! This sample uses a color gradation from white all the way out to blue. You could use your favorite side of the color wheel. If you don't have a color wheel, you can find one online or use C&T Publishing's Essential Color Wheel Companion. It's a wonderful tool, and it's practically a must for this project. Make sure that whatever color wheel you use, it has distinctions for the colors that fall between the primary and secondary colors.

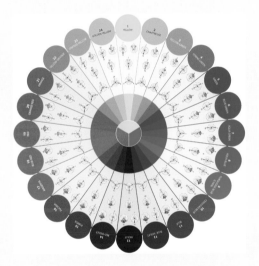

It's best to stay on one side of the color wheel with this project. You will want to move from one color in the wheel to the next and transition using the colors that fall in between. For example, yellow and green are next to each other on the color wheel, but the colors that fall in between them are green-yellow and yellow-green. A yellow that leans green is a yellow-green; a green that leans yellow is a green-yellow. A blue that leans green is a blue-green, and a green that leans blue is a green-blue. It's a great way to practice color transitioning.

MATERIALS

White solid: Scrap large enough to yield 2 squares 4½˝ × 4½˝

Yellow print: Small scraps of 12 different prints, 4 large enough to yield a 4½˝ × 4½˝ square and 8 large enough to yield a 3½˝ × 3½˝ square

Yellow-green print: Small scraps of 8 different prints, 2 large enough to yield a 4½˝ × 4½˝ square and 6 large enough to yield a 3½˝ × 3½˝ square

Green-yellow print: Small scraps of 16 different prints, 4 large enough to yield a 4½˝ × 4½˝ square and 12 large enough to yield a 3½˝ × 3½˝ square

Green print: Small scraps of 16 different prints, 6 large enough to yield a 4½˝ × 4½˝ square and 10 large enough to yield a 3½˝ × 3½˝ square

Green-blue print: Small scraps of 12 different prints, 3 large enough to yield a 4½˝ × 4½˝ square and 9 large enough to yield a 3½˝ × 3½˝ square

Blue-green print: Small scraps of 10 different prints, 5 large enough to yield a 4½˝ × 4½˝ square and 5 large enough to yield a 3½˝ × 3½˝ square

Blue print: Small scraps of 8 different prints, 2 large enough to yield a 4½˝ × 4½˝ square and 6 large enough to yield a 3½˝ × 3½˝ square

Binding: ⅜ yard

Backing: ⅝ yard

Batting: 22˝ × 45˝

CUTTING

Tip It is helpful to organize your squares according to color and to label them. It can be hard to remember what you chose for green-blue or blue-green. Sometimes there are subtle differences.

White solid

• Cut 2 squares 4½˝ × 4½˝.

Yellow print

• Cut 4 squares 4½˝ × 4½˝.

• Cut 8 squares 3½˝ × 3½˝.

Yellow-green print

• Cut 2 squares 4½˝ × 4½˝.

• Cut 6 squares 3½˝ × 3½˝.

Green-yellow print

• Cut 4 squares 4½˝ × 4½˝.

• Cut 12 squares 3½˝ × 3½˝.

Green print

• Cut 6 squares 4½˝ × 4½˝.

• Cut 10 squares 3½˝ × 3½˝.

Green-blue print

• Cut 3 squares 4½˝ × 4½˝.

• Cut 9 squares 3½˝ × 3½˝.

Blue-green print

• Cut 5 squares 4½˝ × 4½˝.

• Cut 5 squares 3½˝ × 3½˝.

Blue print

• Cut 2 squares 4½˝ × 4½˝.

• Cut 6 squares 3½˝ × 3½˝.

Binding

• Cut 4 strips 2½˝ × width of fabric.

Make the Half-Square Triangles

Refer to Making Half-Square Triangles (page 8).

Join the 4½˝ × 4½˝ squares together in pairs, right sides together, using the following color combinations.

1. Join a blue-green square to a blue square. Repeat 1 time for a total of 2 pairs.

2. Join a blue-green square to a green-blue square.

3. Join a blue-green square to a blue-green square.

4. Join a green-blue square to a green square. Repeat 1 time for a total of 2 pairs.

5. Join a green square to a green-yellow square. Repeat 3 more times for a total of 4 pairs.

6. Join a yellow-green square to a yellow square. Repeat 1 time for a total of 2 pairs.

7. Join a yellow square to a white square. Repeat 1 time for a total of 2 pairs.

Pressing and Squaring

1. Press the half-square triangles open, pressing the seam allowance to the darker fabric.

2. Square the half-square triangles to 3½˝ using a 3½˝ acrylic template. Make certain that the center diagonal line of the template rests on the seamline.

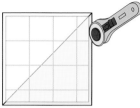

Construct the Columns

Tip It is helpful to have a design wall or a spot on a table to arrange the squares so that they don't get disturbed. This will also help you to see the beautiful transition of the colors.

1. Arrange the runner in 14 columns of 6 units each, referencing the illustration for fabric placement.

2. Stitch the units together from the top of each column to the bottom.

3. Follow the direction of the pressing arrows. See How to Press for Success (page 9) for discussion on pressing seam allowances.

4. Stitch the columns together, using the runner assembly diagram as a reference.

Finishing

Layer the top, batting, and backing. Quilt and bind in the desired manner.

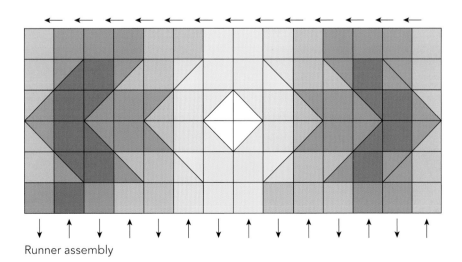

Runner assembly

Father's Day Dinner

Finished table runner: 12½″ × 52″

I don't know anyone who hasn't saved neckties, thinking that they are going to make something with them. This project is completely fun and modern—it combines the lovely silk of the neckties with the strength and great look of linen. Silk is one of the strongest fibers known to man, and linen is also strong. You don't have to worry about babying this table runner. Once it's quilted, you can throw it in the wash on a delicate cycle, hang to dry, and not worry about a thing.

MATERIALS

Assorted silk ties: 10

Gray linen: ⅛ yard (I used Grey Essex by Robert Kaufman Fabrics.)

Natural linen: ⅝ yard (I used Natural Essex by Robert Kaufman Fabrics.)

Woven fusible interfacing: 20″ wide, 1½ yards

Binding: ⅜ yard

Backing: 1 yard

Batting: 16″ × 56″

CUTTING

Gray linen

- Cut 1 strip 6″ × width of fabric; subcut 1 rectangle 6″ × 2½″, 2 rectangles 6″ × 2″, 4 rectangles 4″ × 2″, and 5 rectangles 4″ × 1½″.

Natural linen

- Cut 1 strip 12½″ × width of fabric; subcut 2 rectangles 12½″ × 4½″, 6 rectangles 12½″ × 1½″, 2 rectangles 6″ × 3″, 2 rectangles 6″ × 2½″, and 2 rectangles 6″ × 2″.

- Cut 1 strip 4″ × width of fabric; subcut 2 rectangles 4″ × 3½″, 3 rectangles 4″ × 2½″, 2 rectangles 4″ × 2″, and 5 rectangles 4″ × 1½″.

Binding

- Cut 4 strips 2½″ × width of fabric.

Tip I like to mix it up a little with my binding strips. Sometimes, like with this runner, I'll find coordinating fabric from my stash, cut a short 2½″ strip, and add it in with the binding. It just jazzes it up a little.

Prepare the Neckties

1. Using a seam ripper, take apart each necktie. Remove the inner interfacing and remove any fabric that isn't part of the main fabric by tearing out the seams.

There is a lot of viable fabric in a necktie. This is a really large piece of fabric.

2. Using the silk setting on your iron, iron the tie flat. Test the iron's temperature on a small part of the silk in an area that won't yield much fabric.

3. Lay the most usable part of the necktie— the part with the most fabric—onto the woven fusible interfacing, and trace around the tie with a marking pencil.

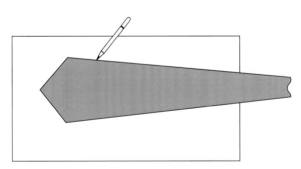

4. Cut the woven fusible interfacing on the lines that were drawn.

5. Apply the fusible side of the woven fusible interfacing to the wrong side of the silk tie fabric. Iron it to the silk following the manufacturer's instructions.

6. Repeat Steps 1–5 for all the neckties.

7. Using a rotary cutter and ruler, square up the neckties into large usable pieces, as shown.

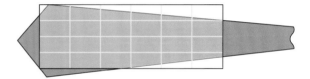

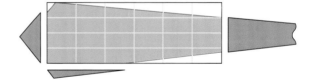

8. From the prepared tie fabrics, cut the following pieces:

2 rectangles 3˝ × 6˝

7 rectangles 2½˝ × 6˝

6 rectangles 3˝ × 4˝

10 rectangles 2½˝ × 4˝

4 rectangles 2˝ × 4˝

Construction

The runner is assembled in 9 pieced columns, plus sashing rectangles of natural linen. 6 columns are 4″ wide, and 3 columns are 6″ wide. The columns are referenced from left to right. For additional help, see the photo of the runner (page 18).

PIECE THE 4″ COLUMNS

Column 1

1. Arrange the following in a column:

2½″ × 4″ necktie rectangle

2½″ × 4″ natural linen rectangle

2″ × 4″ necktie rectangle

1½″ × 4″ gray linen rectangle

2½″ × 4″ natural linen rectangle

3″ × 4″ necktie rectangle

1½″ × 4″ natural linen rectangle

2. Sew together in order.

3. Trim the column to 4″ × 12½″.

4. Label as "column 1."

5. Continue in this manner to create a total of 6 columns, each 4″ wide.

Column 2

1½″ × 4″ gray linen rectangle

2½″ × 4″ necktie rectangle

3½″ × 4″ natural linen rectangle

3″ × 4″ necktie rectangle

2″ × 4″ gray linen rectangle

2½″ × 4″ necktie rectangle

Column 4

2½″ × 4″ necktie rectangle

1½″ × 4″ natural linen rectangle

3″ × 4″ necktie rectangle

1½″ × 4″ natural linen rectangle

2½″ × 4″ necktie rectangle

2″ × 4″ gray linen rectangle

2½″ × 4″ necktie rectangle

Column 6

2″ × 4″ necktie rectangle

2″ × 4″ natural linen rectangle

2½″ × 4″ necktie rectangle

2″ × 4″ gray linen rectangle

3″ × 4″ necktie rectangle

2″ × 4″ natural linen rectangle

2″ × 4″ necktie rectangle

Column 8

1½″ × 4″ gray linen rectangle

3½″ × 4″ natural linen rectangle

2½″ × 4″ necktie rectangle

1½″ × 4″ natural linen rectangle

3″ × 4″ necktie rectangle

1½″ × 4″ gray linen rectangle

2″ × 4″ necktie rectangle

Column 9

1½″ × 4″ natural linen rectangle

2½″ × 4″ necktie rectangle

2″ × 4″ gray linen rectangle

2½″ × 4″ necktie rectangle

3″ × 4″ necktie rectangle

2½″ × 4″ natural linen rectangle

1½″ × 4″ gray linen rectangle

PIECE THE 6″ COLUMNS

These are constructed in the exact same manner as the 4″ columns.

Column 3

2½″ × 6″ necktie rectangle

2½″ × 6″ natural linen rectangle

2½″ × 6″ necktie rectangle

2½″ × 6″ gray linen rectangle

3″ × 6″ necktie rectangle

2″ × 6″ natural linen rectangle

Column 5

2½″ × 6″ natural linen rectangle

2½″ × 6″ necktie rectangle

2″ × 6″ gray linen rectangle

2½″ × 6″ necktie rectangle

3″ × 6″ natural linen rectangle

2½″ × 6″ necktie rectangle

Column 7

2½″ × 6″ necktie rectangle

3″ × 6″ natural linen rectangle

2½″ × 6″ necktie rectangle

2″ × 6″ natural linen rectangle

3″ × 6″ necktie rectangle

2″ × 6″ gray linen rectangle

ADD VERTICAL SASHING RECTANGLES

Tip Make certain all columns are squared to 12½″ in length before adding the sashing rectangles.

1. Arrange the columns in numerical order from left to right.

2. Between columns 1 and 2, stitch a 1½″ × 12½″ rectangle of the natural linen. Press the seam allowances toward the 1½″ rectangle.

3. Add a second 1½″ × 12½″ rectangle of the natural linen to the right edge of column 2.

4. Add column 3 to the previously constructed unit, and press the seam allowance toward the 1½″ rectangle.

5. Refer to the photo (page 18) for the layout of the rest of the columns and the sashing rectangles, using the 4½″ and 1½″ rectangles as shown.

6. Press all seam allowances toward the vertical sashing rectangles.

FINISHING

Layer the top, batting, and backing. Quilt and bind in the desired manner.

Shattered

Finished table runner: 15½″ × 45½″

We've all heard about the traditional quilt block that is called Broken Dishes. Its simplicity has kept it around as a favorite for many years. I tend to gravitate toward dishes that are metallic. I love any fine china that has gold filigree or gold edging. All the fabrics in this table runner have some metallic in them. The dishes are broken and then broken again.

For help with determining which fabrics are light, dark, and medium, see *The Theory of Lights, Darks, and Mediums* (page 10). Here is a photo of the runner taken with the grayscale setting on my camera. Can you see which fabrics are light, dark, and medium?

MATERIALS

Light metallic prints: 4 fat quarters (18″ × 22″) or scraps, enough to yield 28 squares 5½″ × 5½″

Medium metallic prints: 4 fat quarters or scraps, enough to yield 28 squares 5½″ × 5½″

Dark metallic prints: 4 fat quarters or scraps, enough to yield 28 squares 5½″ × 5½″

Binding: ⅜ yard

Backing: ¾ yard

Batting: 18″ × 48″

fast2cut Simple Square Templates by Judy Gauthier (by C&T Publishing), sizes 3½″, 4½″, and 5½″

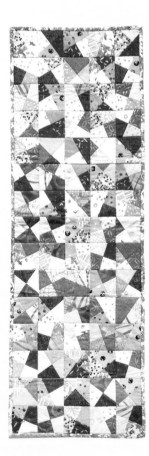

NOTE • The acrylic templates are used to create the squares and to square up the blocks once they are finished. They work incredibly well, especially if you are using scraps.

CUTTING

Light metallic prints

- Cut 28 squares 5½˝ × 5½˝.

Medium metallic prints

- Cut 28 squares 5½˝ × 5½˝.

Dark metallic prints

- Cut 28 squares 5½˝ × 5½˝.

Binding

- Cut 4 strips 2½˝ × width of fabric.

NOTE • There will be extra squares cut for this table runner. This is so that you will have extra if you make an error. It's also because you may decide, for an interesting effect, that you want to add more of one intensity than another to the finished product.

Pair the Fabrics

1. Pair a dark square with a light square, right sides together. Repeat to make a total of 14 light/dark pairs. Label the units "light/dark" and set aside.

2. Pair a dark square with a medium square, right sides together. Repeat to make a total of 14 dark/medium pairs. Label the units "dark/medium" and set aside.

3. Pair a medium square with a light square, right sides together. Repeat to make a total of 14 medium/light pairs. Label the units "medium/light" and set aside.

Make the Half-Square Triangles

1. Follow Making Half-Square Triangles (page 8) to make half-square triangle units using all the paired fabrics. There should be 28 half-square triangle units from each grouping.

2. Press the seam allowances toward the darker fabrics.

3. Continue to keep the units in piles that are separate from each other, labeled with "light/dark," "dark/medium," and "medium/light."

Make the Quarter-Square Triangles

1. Choose a light/dark half-square triangle unit and a dark/medium half-square triangle unit.

2. On one of the half-square triangle units, place a quilting ruler from one corner to the opposite corner, not along the stitching line but perpendicular to it.

3. Cut the unit in half along this diagonal line.

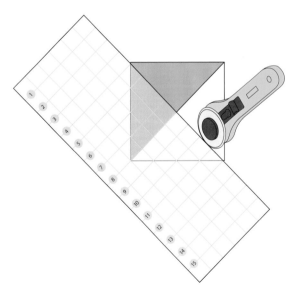

4. Repeat for the other half-square triangle unit.

5. Join these 4 pieces to create 2 quarter-square triangle units.

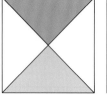

6. Press the seam allowances to one side.

NOTE • When the half-square triangle units are cut in half on the diagonal and paired with another unit that was cut on the diagonal, the seam allowances may not be able to nest when joining them together. It is helpful to place a pin in the ditch where the seam allowances match up prior to sewing them together to keep the seam allowances from working themselves away from each other.

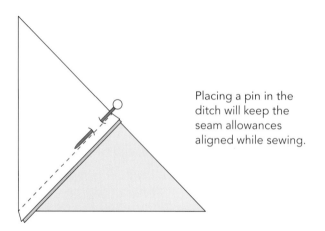

Placing a pin in the ditch will keep the seam allowances aligned while sewing.

7. Place the 3½˝ template over the quarter-square triangle unit.

8. Tilt it at any angle or move it over to one side or the other.

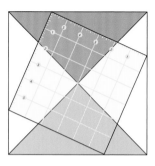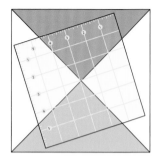

9. Trim around the 3½˝ template with a rotary cutter so that the block looks wonky and unbalanced.

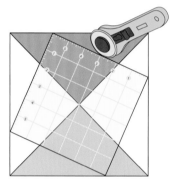

10. Repeat Steps 1–9 for the rest of the half-square triangle blocks. Vary the combinations of lights, mediums, and darks at random, creating quarter-square triangle blocks.

Assemble the Runner

1. Arrange the blocks in 15 rows of 5 blocks each, in a balanced manner with the lights, mediums, and darks evenly distributed.

2. Sew the rows of 5 blocks. Press the seam allowances in the direction of the pressing arrows.

3. Stitch the 15 rows together. Press the seam allowances in one direction.

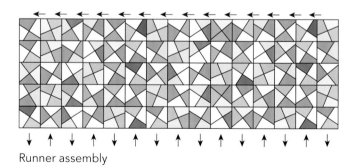

Runner assembly

Finishing

Layer the top, batting, and backing. Quilt and bind in the desired manner.

Hippity-Hop to the Candy Shop

Finished table runner: 16½″ × 52½″

Clean, bright, fresh, *and* modern *describe this table runner. Simplicity in design can be deceiving. Are you up for a challenge? This is not hard, but be careful not to stretch the fabrics!*

Sometimes you need to handle your pieces like they were a delicate piecrust. Imagine you are making a pie, and you have to transfer the crust over to the pan after using your rolling pin to roll it out. It's incredibly tender, and you don't want it to tear. That's how you need to handle things that are on the bias. And please—don't use your iron like a rolling pin!

NOTE • Use a scant ¼″ seam allowance with this one.

MATERIALS

Pink solid: ⅛ yard

Turquoise solid: ⅛ yard

Green solid: ⅛ yard

Red solid: ⅛ yard

White solid: ¾ yard

Woven fusible interfacing: 20″ wide, ⅝ yard

Binding: ⅜ yard (I inserted a bit of print just for fun.)

Backing: ⅞ yard

Batting: 20″ × 56″

CUTTING

Pink, turquoise, green, and red solids

From each color:

• Cut 2 strips 1½″ × width of fabric.

White solid

• Cut 1 strip 16½″ × width of fabric; subcut 9 rectangles 16½″ × 4½″.

• Cut 1 strip 4½″ × width of fabric; subcut 8 rectangles 4½″ × 2½″ and 8 squares 2⅞″ × 2⅞″.

Woven fusible interfacing

• Cut 2 rectangles 8½″ × 22″.

Binding

• Cut 4 strips 2½″ × width of fabric.

Make the Strip Sets

1. Arrange 4 colored strips in the following order: pink, green, turquoise, and red.

2. Stitch the 4 colored strips together along the long edges. Press the seam allowances in the same direction.

3. Measure the strip set to find the center and cut in half.

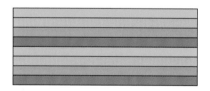

4. Place together the strip sets that have been cut so that there are 8 strips, making certain that the colors alternate. Do not sew 2 of the same colors together. Stitch together. Press the seam allowance in the same direction as the rest.

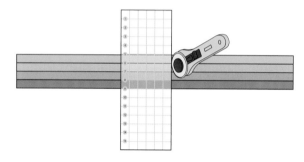

5. Press the strip set from the right side, making certain that there are no "lips" of fabric and that all seams are flat.

6. Repeat Steps 1–5 using the second set of 1½″ strips.

7. Lay the strip sets wrong side up. Place a woven fusible interfacing rectangle with the fusible side against the wrong side of the strip set. Following the manufacturer's directions, press so that the interfacing is adhered to the strip sets.

Make the Diagonal Cuts

1. Lay one strip set right side up on a cutting mat, with the straight edge of the bottom strip along a straight line on the cutting mat.

2. Using the 45° angle on a cutting ruler, lay the ruler on the strip set at a 45° angle, with the ruler slanted to the right along the right edge of the strip set. Make certain that the ruler covers all strips.

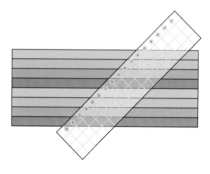

3. Cut along the edge of the ruler, yielding a 45°-angle cut.

4. Move the ruler so that the newly cut edge is at the 2½″ line. Cut a 2½″ strip that is at a 45° angle.

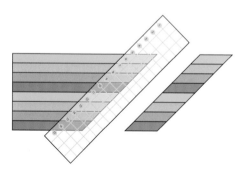

5. Continue in this manner, cutting a total of 4 strips each 2½″ wide.

6. Repeat with the second strip set.

NOTE • At this point, the bias edges of the strips are exposed. Even though there is interfacing on the back, you must be very, very careful while handling them so that they don't stretch. Remember to treat them like delicate piecrust!

Construct the Runner

1. Cut the 8 white squares 2⅞″ × 2⅞″ into half-square triangles by laying a cutting ruler on the squares and cutting across a diagonal line.

2. Add white half-square triangles to the ends of the colored strips. Open out and press the seam allowance toward the colored strip, being careful not to stretch.

3. Trim the triangles to 2½″ wide, matching the width of the strips.

4. Lay all 8 strips right sides up in the same color order.

5. Stitch a 2½″ × 4½″ white rectangle to 4 of the strips at the pink end. These will be called *unit P*.

6. Repeat this for the other 4 strips on the red end of the strip. These will be called *unit R*.

7. Press the seam allowance toward the rectangles.

8. Trim all these strip units to 16½″ at the white rectangle end.

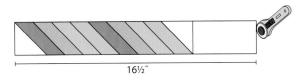

16½″

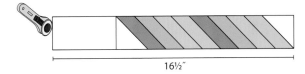

16½″

9. Referring to the table runner photo (page 25), arrange the 4½″ × 16½″ white rectangles and pieced strips side by side. Alternate P units with R units.

10. Stitch the white rectangles and pieced strips together. Press the seam allowances toward the colored strips.

Tip When sewing strips or triangles where there is a bias edge, it is often helpful to keep the pieces with the bias against the feed dogs or on the bottom of the two layers. This will help ease any stretch that may have occurred.

Finishing

Layer the top, batting, and backing. Quilt and bind in the desired manner.

What Came First?

Finished table runner: 15½″ × 48½″

I feel like every kitchen needs a good chicken accessory. It's such a staple in most kitchens! After all, we eat eggs and we eat chicken; it's natural. These brightly colored chickens can be made to match any decor.

MATERIALS

Brown: ½ yard for chicken bodies and triangles

Yellow: ⅛ yard for wing and comb

Blue: ⅛ yard for wing and comb

Red: ⅛ yard for wing, comb, and wattles

Yellow dot: Scraps for beaks

Off-white: ¾ yard for background

Binding: ⅜ yard

Backing: ⅞ yard

Batting: 19″ × 52″

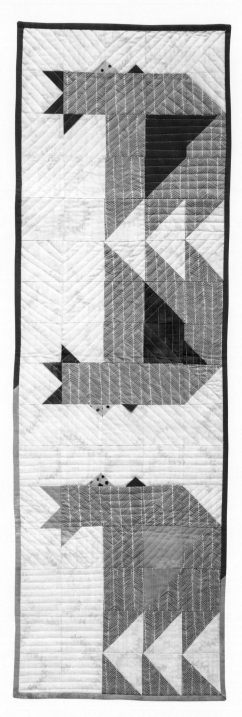

CUTTING

Brown

- Cut 11 squares 4½″ × 4½″.
- Cut 21 squares 3½″ × 3½″.

Yellow and blue

From each color:

- Cut 1 square 4½″ × 4½″.
- Cut 1 square 3½″ × 3½″.
- Cut 1 square 2″ × 2″.
- Cut 3 squares 1½″ × 1½″.

Red

- Cut 1 square 4½″ × 4½″.
- Cut 1 square 3½″ × 3½″.
- Cut 1 square 2″ × 2″.
- Cut 6 squares 1½″ × 1½″.

Yellow dot

- Cut 6 squares 1″ × 1″.

Off-white

- Cut 8 squares 4½″ × 4½″.
- Cut 38 squares 3½″ × 3½″.

Binding

- Cut 4 strips 2½″ × width of fabric.

Make the Half-Square Triangles

1. Pair 8 brown squares 4½″ × 4½″ with 8 off-white squares 4½″ × 4½″.

2. Following the instructions for Making Half-Square Triangles (page 8), make 16 half-square triangle units.

3. Press the seam allowances toward the brown fabric.

4. Pair 1 yellow square 4½″ × 4½″ with 1 brown square 4½″ × 4½″.

5. Pair 1 blue square 4½″ × 4½″ with 1 brown square 4½″ × 4½″.

6. Pair 1 red square 4½″ × 4½″ with 1 brown square 4½″ × 4½″.

7. Make 2 half-square triangle units of each color pairing. Only one of each will be used. Press the seam allowances toward the darker fabrics and trim to 3½″ × 3½″.

NOTE • The leftover half-square triangle units can be used on the back of the table runner if so desired. Many quilters use extra units and blocks to dress up the backs of the quilt or runner.

Make the Comb Units

1. Lay a 1½″ × 1½″ yellow square on a 3½″ × 3½″ off-white square in one corner, right sides together and aligning the edges.

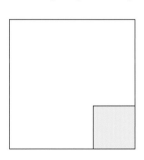

2. With a marking pen, mark a diagonal line from one outside corner to the opposite outside corner.

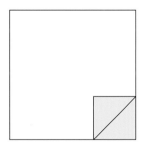

3. Stitch along the outside edge of the line.

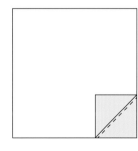

4. Trim off the outside corner of the yellow fabric, leaving a ¼″ seam allowance and also leaving the background fabric underneath untrimmed.

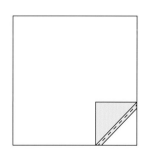

5. Press the yellow square downward toward the background fabric.

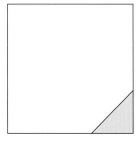

6. Repeat Steps 1–5 to make a red unit and a blue unit. Set these aside.

7. Repeat Steps 1–5 to make another yellow, green, and red unit.

8. Add a second yellow square to one yellow unit on the adjacent corner. In the same way, add a second square to one each of the blue and red units.

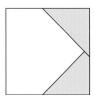 

Make the Lower Wing Sections

1. Lay a 2″ × 2″ yellow square on a 3½″ × 3½″ off-white square, right sides together, matching the corners and aligning the sides.

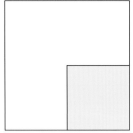

2. Follow Make the Comb Units, Steps 2–5 (page 29).

3. Repeat Steps 1 and 2 to make a blue and red lower wing section.

Make the Beak Units

1. With right sides together, lay a 1″ × 1″ yellow-dot square on the corner of a 3½″ × 3½″ off-white square.

2. Follow Make the Comb Units, Steps 2–5 (page 29).

3. Repeat Steps 1 and 2 for a total of 6 beak units.

Assemble the Runner

1. This table runner is assembled in columns, and then the columns are sewn together. There are 16 columns of 5 units each. Use the photo of the runner (page 28) as a reference.

Tip It is helpful to label the columns from 1 to 16 when assembling them, or you can use a design wall. Remember: The blue chicken is facing the opposite direction of the other two chickens.

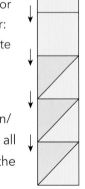

2. For column 1, sew together 2 off-white squares 3½″ × 3½″ and 3 brown/off-white half-square triangles. Press all seam allowances in the direction of the arrows.

3. Sew the other columns, referring to the photo for the unit order and placement. Alternate direction for pressing seam allowances.

4. To make a wattle, fold a 1½″ × 1½″ red square diagonally, wrong sides together. Press. Fold the square a second time, from the center of the triangle to the point, bringing the 2 opposite points together. Press. Make 3.

5. Stitch the columns together and press the seam allowances to one side. When sewing column 5 to column 6, insert a wattle into the seam allowance, with the point on the inside of the 2 columns. Stitch into the seam. When the columns are opened out to press, the wattle should be sticking out freely.

6. Repeat Step 5 for the next 2 chickens between columns 7 and 8, and columns 15 and 16.

Finishing

Layer the top, batting, and backing. Quilt and bind in the desired manner.

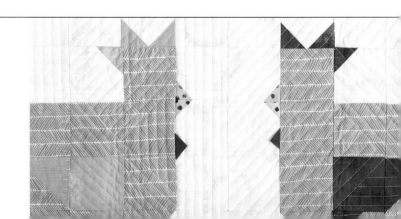

Confetti

Finished table runner: 12½″ × 30½″

Here's a fun runner by guest maker Eliane Bergmann. Eliane has a bright, sunny personality. It's no surprise that she made a runner that would chase any blues away! This can be made by beginning and experienced quilters alike, and is sure to put a smile on your face every time you see it on your table.

MATERIALS

Assorted scraps of 8 colors (teal, light aqua, dark turquoise, magenta, orange, pink, yellow, and green), each large enough to yield 6 squares 2″ × 2″

White: ½ yard

Binding: ⅓ yard

Backing: ½ yard

Batting: 16″ × 34″

CUTTING

Assorted scraps

From each color:

• Cut 6 squares 2″ × 2″.

White

• Cut 4 strips 2½″ × width of fabric; subcut 30 squares 2½″ × 2½″, 2 rectangles 2½″ × 12½″, 32 rectangles 2½″ × 1″, and 32 rectangles 2½″ × ¾″.

• Cut 2 strips 2″ × width of fabric; subcut 32 rectangles 2″ × 1″ and 32 rectangles 2″ × ¾″.

Binding

• Cut 3 strips 2½″ × width of fabric.

Construction

Separate the colored squares into 2 stacks: Place 2 of each color into a stack for the A blocks and 4 of each color into a stack for the B blocks.

MAKE THE A BLOCKS

1. Stitch 2 white rectangles 2″ × ¾″ to each colored square on opposite sides.

2. Press the seam allowances toward the square.

3. Stitch a 2½″ × ¾″ white rectangle to each remaining side of each unit. Press the seam allowance toward the square. Make 16.

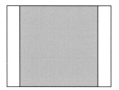
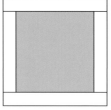

Block A

MAKE THE B BLOCKS

1. Stitch a 2″ × 1″ white rectangle to a colored square. Press the seam allowance toward the square.

2. Stitch a 2½″ × 1″ white rectangle to an adjacent side of the colored square. Press the seam allowance toward the square. Make 32.

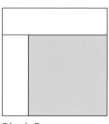

Block B

ASSEMBLE THE RUNNER

1. Follow the assembly diagram to arrange the blocks and white squares.

2. Rotate the B blocks so that they are not all lying in the same direction.

3. Stitch the blocks and squares together in 13 rows of 6. Follow the arrows for pressing seam allowances.

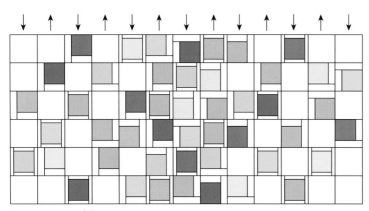

Runner assembly

4. Stitch the 13 rows together and press the seam allowances all in the same direction.

5. Stitch a 2½″ × 12½″ white rectangle to each end of the runner. Press the seam allowances toward the center of the runner.

FINISHING

Layer the top, batting, and backing. Quilt and bind in the desired manner.

Frequency

Finished table runner: 12½˝ × 36½˝

This runner is made using fabric that I designed for Ink & Arrow for QT Fabrics. I love vintage transistor radios; they give me such good memories of my childhood. If you are too young to have those memories, they are fun for a vintage look. This runner would look great using any fabric.

MATERIALS

Black: 1 fat quarter (18˝ × 22˝)

Aqua: 1 fat quarter (18˝ × 22˝)

Main print: ¼ yard

Binding: ⅓ yard

Backing: ½ yard

Batting: 15˝ × 40˝

CUTTING

Black and aqua

From each color:

- Cut 2 strips 2˝ × 22˝; subcut 4 rectangles 2˝ × 5˝ and 6 rectangles 2˝ × 3½˝.

- Cut 6 squares 3½˝ × 3½˝.

Main print

- Cut 3 rectangles 6½˝ × 12½˝.

Binding

- Cut 3 strips 2½˝ × width of fabric.

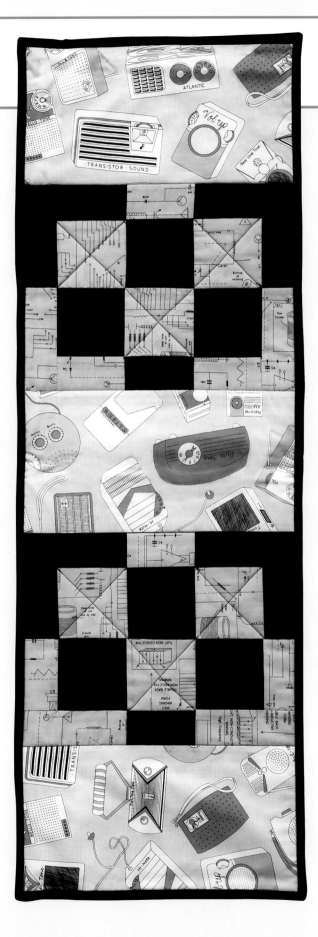

Make the Units

1. Stitch a 2˝ × 3½˝ aqua rectangle to a 3½˝ × 3½˝ black square. Press the seam allowance to the black fabric. Make 6.

Tip It is helpful to chain piece the rectangles to the squares. It saves a lot of time and thread.

2. Stitch a 2˝ × 5˝ aqua rectangle to a unit from Step 1. Make 4, being sure that they are sewn in a mirror image. These will be called *black unit A*.

Black unit A

3. The units without the additional rectangle will be called *black unit B*.

Black unit B

4. Repeat Steps 1–3 using the aqua squares and black rectangles. Label these as *aqua unit A* and *aqua unit B*.

Make the Blocks

1. Stitch 2 black units A to opposite sides of an aqua unit B.

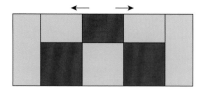

2. Press the seam allowances toward the black units A.

3. Stitch 2 aqua units A to opposite sides of a black unit B.

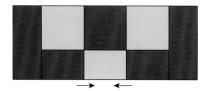

4. Press the seam allowances toward the black unit B.

5. Stitch the 2 large units together along the side with the squares to complete the block.

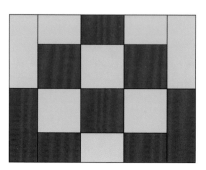

6. Repeat Steps 1–5 to make 2 blocks.

Assemble the Runner

Sew together 3 main-print rectangles 6½˝ × 12½˝ and the 2 blocks along the long edges. Refer to the photo (page 33) for placement and orientation. Press the seam allowances toward the main-print rectangles.

Finishing

Layer the top, batting, and backing. Quilt and bind in the desired manner.

Where All Roads Lead

Finished table runner: 15½″ × 35½″

Where All Roads Lead was created by my quilty BFF, Cathy Roeder! We all have that one person we run to when we want someone to tell us what is right or what is wrong with our project, and Cathy is mine. This runner is simple to sew but has an engaging design. No matter what color scheme you choose, all roads will lead to you feeling very satisfied.

MATERIALS

Large-scale turquoise print: ¼ yard

Medium-scale turquoise print: ¼ yard

Light turquoise blender: ¼ yard

Chartreuse texture: ⅛ yard

White tone-on-tone: ½ yard

Binding: ⅓ yard

Backing: ⅝ yard

Batting: 19″ × 39″

CUTTING

Turquoise prints and blender

From each fabric:

- Cut 2 strips 3″ × width of fabric; subcut 8 rectangles 3″ × 5½″ and 8 squares 3″ × 3″.

Chartreuse texture

- Cut 1 strip 3″ × width of fabric; subcut 4 rectangles 3″ × 5½″ and 4 squares 3″ × 3″.

White tone-on-tone

- Cut 4 strips 3″ × width of fabric; subcut 14 rectangles 3″ × 5½″ and 28 squares 3″ × 3″.

Binding

- Cut 3 strips 2½″ × width of fabric.

Make the Chartreuse Center Column

1. With right sides together, lay a 3″ × 3″ chartreuse square on a 3″ × 5½″ white rectangle, matching the corners and edges.

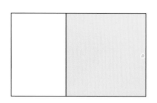

2. Draw a diagonal line on the chartreuse square from the upper right corner to the lower left corner.

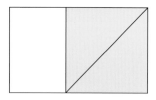

3. Stitch slightly to the outside of the line drawn.

Stitch just to the side of the line.

Tip When making units such as these, where you are stitching on the line and then folding the half-square over onto itself, it is helpful to stitch just on the outside edge of the line in the direction of the fold. That way you are sure to cover the underlying fabric completely.

4. Fold the top square over toward the outside of the rectangle and press.

5. Trim the top square on the underside, leaving the rectangle intact.

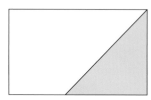

6. In the same way, add a second 3″ × 3″ chartreuse square to the opposite end of the same 3″ × 5½″ white rectangle. This will be called *chartreuse unit A*. Make 2.

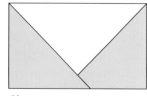

Chartreuse unit A

7. Repeat Steps 1–6 with white squares 3″ × 3″ and chartreuse rectangles 3″ × 5½″. These will be called *chartreuse unit B*.

8. Sew together 2 chartreuse rectangles 3″ × 5½″, 2 chartreuse units A, and 2 chartreuse units B to make the center column. Press all the seam allowances in the direction of the arrows.

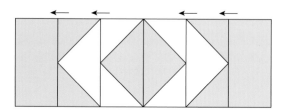

Make the Turquoise Columns

Repeat Make the Chartreuse Center Column, Steps 1–8 with each of the turquoise rectangles and squares. Make 2 columns with each print.

Assemble the Runner

Arrange all the columns in the correct order. Rotate the columns so that the seams alternate directions. Stitch all the columns together, pressing all seams in the same direction.

Finishing

Layer the top, batting, and backing. Quilt and bind in the desired manner.

Hexie Star

Finished table runner: 16½″ × 56″

This table runner idea came to me when I was thinking of patterns within patterns. It would also be a great quilt. But for now, it's a table runner!

MATERIALS

Scraps of 7 different prints

White: 1½ yards

Binding: ⅜ yard

Backing: 1 yard

Batting: 20″ × 60″

Clearview Triangle 60° Acrylic Ruler—10″ (by C&T Publishing)

fast2cut Simple Square Templates by Judy Gauthier (by C&T Publishing), sizes 3½″, 4½″, and 5½″

NOTE • The 3½″ square template is used to cut a perfect 3½″ square from any odd-shaped scraps that are used in the construction of the runner.

CUTTING

Scrap 1

• Cut 6 rectangles 3½″ × 5½″.

Scraps 2–7

From each print:

• Cut 2 squares 3½″ × 3½″ and 1 rectangle 1½″ × 3½″.

Binding

• Cut 4 strips 2½″ × width of fabric.

White

• Cut 4 strips 6½″ × width of fabric; subcut 36 rectangles 6½″ × 4½″.

• Cut 3 strips 3½″ × width of fabric; subcut 12 rectangles 3½″ × 5½″, 6 squares 3½″ × 3½″, and 12 rectangles 3½″ × 1½″.

• Cut 4 triangles that measure 8¾″ from top to bottom.

NOTE • The Clearview Triangle 60° Acrylic Ruler is a pointed-tip ruler; therefore you add ¾″ to the finished height to determine the cut height. If you are using a blunt-tip 60° triangle ruler, add ½″ to the finished height. The cut height for these triangles would be 8½″.

Make the End Hexagons

1. Sew a 3½″ × 1½″ white rectangle and a 3½″ × 5½″ white rectangle to opposite sides of a 3½″ × 3½″ scrap square. Press the seam allowances toward the scrap square. This is called *unit A*. Make 12.

Unit A

2. Align a 6½″ × 4½″ white rectangle with the left side of unit A, as shown. Sew with right sides together. Repeat to add another 6½″ × 4½″ white rectangle to right side of unit A. Press the seam allowances toward unit A.

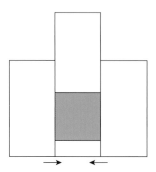

3. Center the 60° pointed-tip triangle ruler on unit A, with the 8¾″ ruler line aligned with the bottom raw edge of the unit. Using a sharp rotary cutter, cut the angled edges, yielding a triangle. If using a blunt-tip ruler, align the 8½″ line on the ruler.

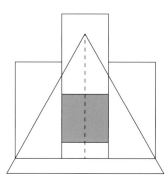

4. Repeat Steps 2 and 3 to make 12 triangles total.

Tip You may save the triangles that are trimmed off of the sides. These triangles can be used for the construction of the other table runner units, substituting them for the 6½″ × 4½″ white rectangles. If you choose to do this, they must be reversed and placed on the opposite sides of unit A. This will be clearer once you have made a couple units.

NOTE • The edges of the triangles are on the bias. These must be handled very delicately. If you desire, you can spray starch on the triangles to keep them from stretching. Handle them like a delicate piecrust!

5. With right sides together, join 2 triangles, matching the seams. Stop stitching ¼˝ from the point. Press the seam allowance to one side.

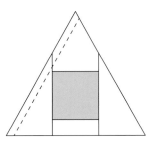

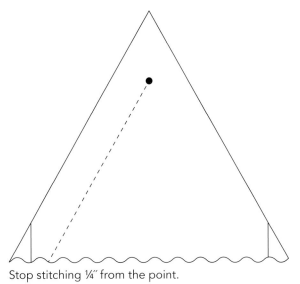

Stop stitching ¼˝ from the point.

6. Add another triangle to the 2 sewn together, matching the seam allowances. Make certain to stop stitching ¼˝ from the top point. Press the seam allowance in the same direction that you chose before.

7. Repeat Steps 5 and 6, sewing together another 3 triangles. Press the seam allowances in the same direction as you did in the first 3.

8. Align the 2 sets of 3 triangles along the straight edge, matching the center seams, and sew together.

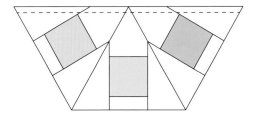

9. Open out and press the seam allowance in the same direction as you pressed all the others. Since you stopped stitching ¼˝ from the point, you should be able to have all the seam allowances lying in the same direction, and the center of all the points should now lie flat.

10. Repeat Steps 5–9 to create a second end hexagon.

Make the Center Hexagon

NOTE • *The center hexagon is made exactly like the end hexagons. Only the placement of the fabrics is different.*

Using 6 scrap rectangles 3½˝ × 1½˝, 6 white squares 3½˝ × 3½˝, and 6 matching 3½˝ × 5½˝ scrap rectangles, follow Make the End Hexagons, Steps 1–8 (previous page and above) to make the center hexagon.

Assemble the Runner

1. Arrange the 3 hexagons side by side. Place 8¾″ white triangles in the spaces in between the hexagons.

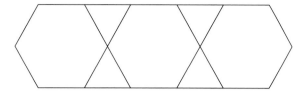

2. With right sides together, stitch an 8¾″ white triangle to the upper right side of the first hexagon. Open out and press toward the hexagon.

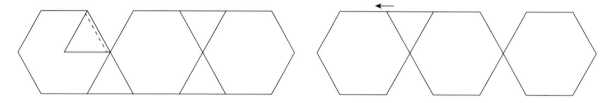

3. Stitch an 8¾″ white triangle to the lower left side of the center hexagon. Open out and press toward the hexagon.

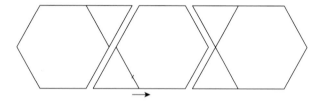

4. Stitch the 2 units together along the unsewn edges of the triangles. Match the seam allowances at the center. Open out and press the seam allowance to either side.

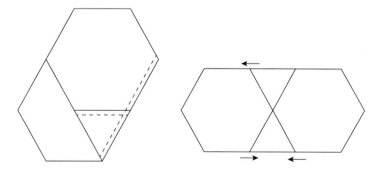

5. Stitch a white triangle to the upper right side of the center hexagon. Stitch a white triangle to the lower left side of the remaining hexagon. Stitch the center hexagon and triangle to the last remaining hexagon and triangle, matching the center seams. Open out and press the seam allowance to either side.

Finishing

Layer the top, batting, and backing. Quilt and bind in the desired manner.

Cross My Heart

Finished table runner: 16½˝ × 46½˝

After returning from a trip to Scotland, I realized how much I love argyle. So I combined my love for argyle with a symbol for love! This runner is not for beginners, but it isn't extremely difficult either. It's well worth the effort.

MATERIALS

Pink prints: ½ yard total or scraps large enough to yield 4 squares 6½˝ × 6½˝ and 8 squares 5½˝ × 5½˝

Mint: ⅛ yard

Mustard: ⅛ yard

Cream: ¾ yard

Binding: ⅜ yard

Backing: ¾ yard

Batting: 20˝ × 50˝

CUTTING

Pink prints

- Cut 4 squares 6½″ × 6½″.

- Cut 8 squares 5½″ × 5½″.

Mint

- Cut 16 squares 2″ × 2″.

Mustard

- Cut 4 strips 1″ × width of fabric; subcut 8 strips 1″ × 16″.

Cream

- Cut 1 strip 6½″ × width of fabric; subcut 4 squares 6½″ × 6½″.

- Cut 3 strips 3½″ × width of fabric; subcut 2 strips 3½″ × 40½″ and 2 strips 3½″ × 16½″.

- Cut 1 strip 2½″ × width of fabric; subcut 8 squares 2½″ × 2½″ and 8 squares 2″ × 2″.

Binding

- Cut 4 strips 2½″ × width of fabric.

Make the Half-Square Triangles

1. Pair 4 pink squares 6½″ × 6½″ with 4 cream squares 6½″ × 6½″.

2. Make 8 half-square triangle units by following the steps in Making Half-Square Triangles (page 8).

3. Square the half-square triangle units to 5½″ × 5½″.

4. Place a 2″ × 2″ mint square right sides together on the pink half of a half-square triangle unit, matching the corners and edges.

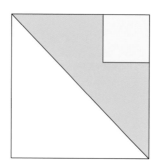

5. Draw a diagonal line across the mint square from the upper left to the lower right corner. Stitch on this line from corner to corner.

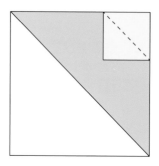

6. Open the mint square to the right side. Fold and press toward the outer corner.

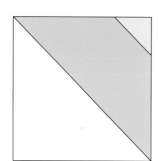

7. Trim the underside of the mint square between the top half and the pink fabric.

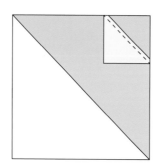

8. Repeat Steps 4–7 for the remainder of the half-square triangles.

Make the Heart Top Units

TOP LEFT UNITS

1. Place a 2″ × 2″ cream square on the upper left corner of a 5½″ × 5½″ pink square. Draw a diagonal line across the cream square from the upper right to the lower left corner.

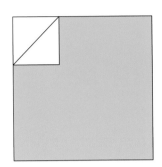

2. Stitch on the line.

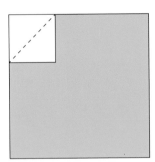

3. Fold the right half of the square out toward the outer corner and press. Trim the underside of the cream square between the top half and the pink fabric.

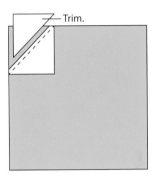

4. Using the same technique, add a 2½″ × 2½″ cream square to the upper right corner of the unit and a 2″ × 2″ mint square to the lower right corner of the unit.

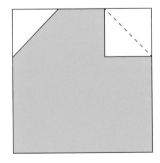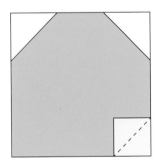

5. Repeat Steps 1–4 to make a total of 4 top left units.

TOP RIGHT UNITS

Repeat Top Left Units, Steps 1–5, except with the mint square placed in the lower left corner to make 4 top right units. Refer to the photo (page 41) for fabric placement.

Make the Hearts

1. Place all 16 heart units wrong side up on a cutting mat. Use the 5½˝ square template to square up the units if needed.

2. Sew a top left unit to a top right unit, being careful to match the points of the cream and mint squares. Press the seam allowance to the left unit. Repeat to make 4 top heart sections.

3. Sew 2 half-square triangles together, being careful to match the points of the mint squares. Press the seam allowance toward the right unit. Repeat to make 4 bottom heart sections.

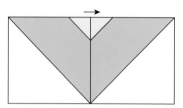

4. Matching seam allowances, sew a top heart section to a bottom heart section. Repeat to create 4 Heart blocks. Press the center seams for 2 hearts toward the bottom heart sections and 2 toward the upper heart sections.

Add the Argyle Stripes

NOTE • You may feel like you need to go and lie down in a dark room with a cool washcloth on your head when you think about cutting into your beautiful Heart blocks, but cut you must! Read this section through before cutting.

1. Lay a quilting ruler across the Heart block from the upper left corner to the lower right corner. Cut the Heart block along the ruler.

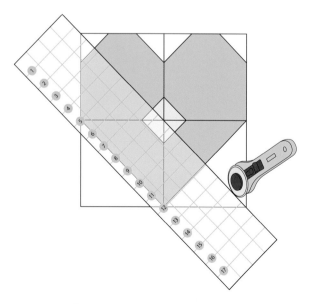

2. Lay a 1˝ × 16˝ mustard strip across one cut half of the heart, right sides together, making sure that the strip extends beyond both ends of the heart.

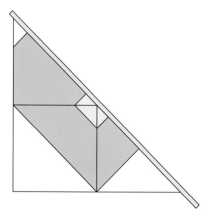

3. Stitch a scant ¼˝ seam along the edge.

Tip You may find the zipper foot on your machine works well to sew this strip to the Heart block.

4. Press the seam allowance toward the strip.

5. Lay the other half of the heart on top of the mustard strip. Be very careful to mark with pins where the edges of the mint square are and the edges of the heart are so that they are aligned when the pieces are sewn. Pin securely or baste.

Tip It may help to sew the pieces with a long basting stitch on your machine before sewing it using a regular-length stitch. This way you can remove the stitches easier if needed.

Tip It works well to use a lightbox under the block to line up the seams. If you don't have a lightbox, a sunny window can work.

6. Stitch using a scant ¼″ seam. Press the seam allowance toward the strip.

7. Lay a quilting ruler across the heart from the upper right corner to the lower left corner, intersecting the previously sewn strip. Cut the Heart block along the ruler.

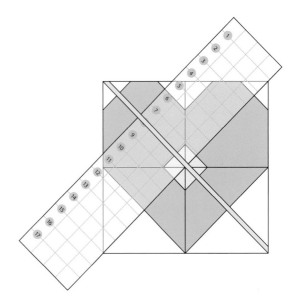

8. Repeat Steps 2–6.

9. Repeat Steps 1–8 for the remaining 3 hearts. Trim the blocks to 10½″ × 10½″ square.

Assemble the Runner

1. Sew 4 Heart blocks together, alternating the direction of the center seam. Press the seams toward either side.

2. Sew a 3½″ × 40½″ cream strip along the top and bottom edges of the Heart blocks. Press the seam allowances toward the strip.

3. Stitch a 3½″ × 16½″ cream strip to each end of the runner. Press the seam allowances toward the strip.

Finishing

Layer the top, batting, and backing. Quilt and bind in the desired manner.

Country Farmhouse

Finished table runner: 14½˝ × 50˝

Nothing says "country farmhouse" like red-and-white gingham and canning jars. This fabric came from a pile that my daughter had left on my doorstep. I took one look at the canning-jar print and knew that it belonged on a kitchen table.

MATERIALS

Main print: ¼ yard

Red gingham: ⅛ yard

White: ⅔ yard

Red prints: Scraps of 12 different prints, each large enough to yield a 3½˝ × 3½˝ square

Binding: ⅓ yard

Backing: 1 yard

Batting: 18˝ × 54˝

CUTTING

Main print

- Cut 1 strip 5½˝ × width of fabric; subcut 7 squares 5½˝ × 5½˝.

Red gingham

- Cut 10 squares 3½˝ × 3½˝.

White

- Cut 2 strips 5½˝ × width of fabric; subcut 10 squares 5½˝ × 5½˝ and 10 squares 2½˝ × 2½˝.

- Cut 6 strips 1½˝ × width of fabric; subcut 12 rectangles 1½˝ × 5½˝, 24 rectangles 1½˝ × 4½˝, and 12 rectangles 1½˝ × 3½˝.

Red prints

- Cut 12 squares 3½˝ × 3½˝.

Binding

- Cut 3 strips 2½˝ × width of fabric.

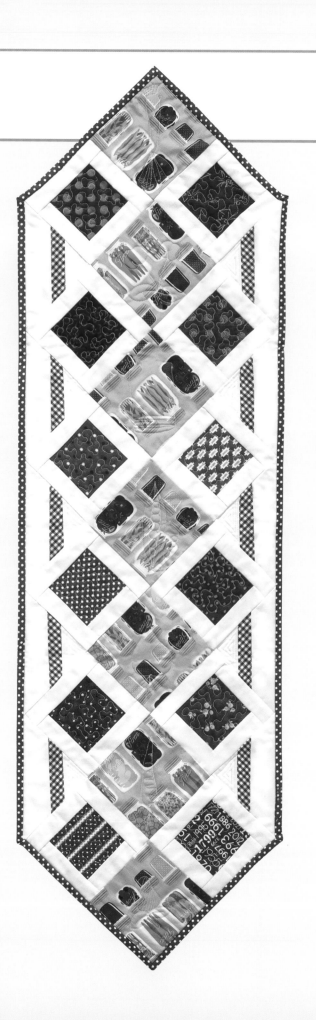

Make the Red Print Units

NOTE • Press all seam allowances toward the red squares.

1. Sew a 1½″ × 3½″ white rectangle to a 3½″ × 3½″ red print square.

2. Sew a 1½″ × 4½″ white rectangle to the adjacent side of the unit.

3. Sew a 1½″ × 4½″ white rectangle to the side opposite the 1½″ × 3½″ rectangle.

4. Sew a 1½″ × 5½″ white rectangle to the remaining side of the red square.

5. Repeat Steps 1–4 for the 11 remaining red print squares.

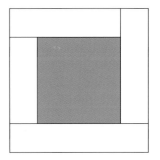

Make the Gingham Stripe Units

1. Draw a diagonal line on the wrong side of each of the 10 gingham squares 3½″ × 3½″.

2. With right sides together, lay a gingham square on a 5½″ × 5½″ white square, matching the corners and edges.

3. Stitch on the line.

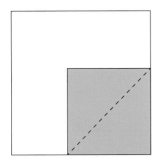

4. Fold the square outward and press. Trim the triangle that is between the top half of the gingham square and the white square, leaving the 5½″ × 5½″ white square untrimmed.

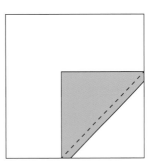

5. Repeat Steps 1–4 for all 10 gingham squares 3½″ × 3½″ and white squares 5½″ × 5½″.

6. Lay a 2½″ × 2½″ white square on the corner of a gingham triangle. Draw a diagonal line across the 2½″ × 2½″ square.

7. Follow Steps 3 and 4 for all 10 gingham squares to complete the gingham stripe units.

Assemble the Runner

1. Sew the first row using a main print square, a red print unit, and a gingham stripe unit.

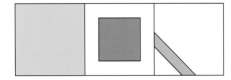

2. Sew the second row using 2 red print units, a main print square, and a gingham stripe unit.

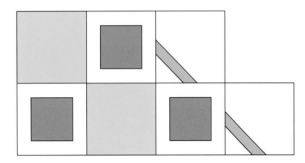

3. Referring to the photo (page 46), sew rows 3–5 using 2 gingham stripe units, 2 red print units, and a main print square in each row.

4. Sew rows 6 and 7 as mirror images of rows 2 and 1.

5. Sew the rows together, referring to the photo and illustrations.

Quilt the Runner

NOTE • When the runner is trimmed, the edges will be on the bias. That is why the runner is quilted before it is trimmed. There will be more stability if it is quilted before trimming.

1. Layer the runner, batting, and backing.

2. Quilt in your favorite manner.

Trim and Bind the Runner

1. Using a ruler and rotary cutter, trim the long edges of the runner, lining the ruler up with the end of the seams.

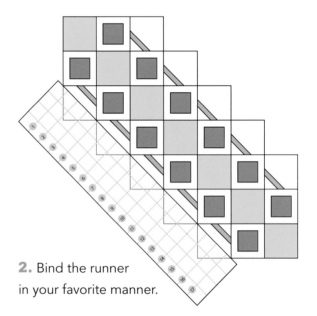

2. Bind the runner in your favorite manner.

Pure Elegance

Finished table topper: 29½″ × 38″

This is more of a table topper than a runner, but I think it's equally beautiful. Some folks have a round table that they want to grace with something homemade, and it's absolutely perfect for that. It would be equally beautiful as a Christmas-tree skirt!

MATERIALS

Cream cotton prints: 14 fat quarters (18″ × 22″) *total, or* scraps of 14 different fabrics, each large enough to yield 3 squares 5½″ × 5½″

Tan felted wool: 1 fat quarter (18″ × 22″)

Fusible interfacing: 20″ wide, ⅜ yard

Binding: ⅜ yard

Backing: 1 yard

Batting: 33″ × 42″

5½″ × 5½″ square template

Ruler that measures ¹⁄₁₆″ increments

CUTTING

Cream cotton prints

From each print:

- Cut 3 squares 5½″ × 5½″.

Tan felted wool

- Cut 7 circles 3½″ in diameter.

Fusible interfacing

- Cut 7 squares 4½″ × 4½″.

Binding

- Cut 4 strips 2½″ × width of fabric.

Make the Half-Rings

1. Pair 3 matching 5½″ × 5½″ cream print squares with 3 squares of a second cream print. Place each pair of squares right sides together.

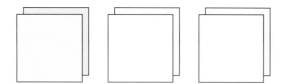

NOTE • It is very important that the same print is on the top layer consistently and the same print is on the bottom consistently. Do not mix them in any of the following steps.

2. Make a mark 1³⁄₁₆″ from the top right corner of the top square in each layered pair and 1³⁄₁₆″ from the lower left corner of the top square in each layered pair. Place the layered pairs on a cutting mat.

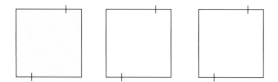

3. Align a long quilting ruler with the marks on the first pair.

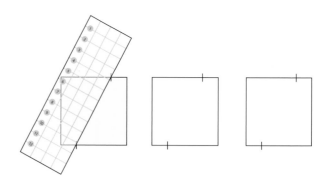

4. Using your rotary cutter, cut along the edge of the ruler. Repeat for all 3 pairs.

5. Keeping the shapes paired with right sides together, stitch along the long straight edge of each pair.

Tip I like to take all the paired shapes with me right to the sewing machine and chain piece them. It saves a lot of thread.

6. Open the shapes out. Press the seam allowances open.

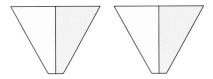

7. Stitch one wedge to another. Open out and press the seam allowances open.

8. Stitch a third wedge to the pair. Press the seam allowances open.

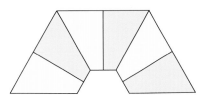

9. Repeat Steps 7 and 8 to make a second half-ring of the same fabric combination. Do not stitch the halves together, but place them together to keep them in order.

10. Repeat Steps 1–9 for the remaining 5½˝ × 5½˝ cream squares.

Make the Rows

1. Lay 2 different half-rings right sides up next to each other, with the long edge of one on the bottom and the long edge of the other on top.

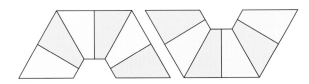

2. Place them right sides together, matching the edges of the wedges, and stitch.

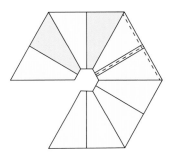

3. Open out and press the seam allowance open.

4. Repeat Steps 1–3 to join a third half-ring to the row.

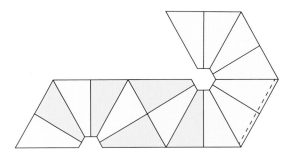

5. Place the matching half-ring of the center half-ring right sides together with the center half-ring. Stitch. Open out and press the seam allowance open.

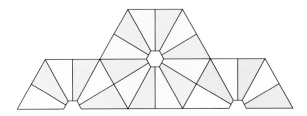

6. Make and join the remaining rows using the remaining half-rings, referring to the photo (page 49) for reference.

Reinforce the Center Openings

1. Turn the topper over, wrong side up.

2. Place a 4½″ × 4½″ fusible interfacing square over each opening in the rings.

3. Press the squares over the openings.

NOTE • Make certain to cover the underside of the opening with a nonstick pressing cloth to prevent the fusible interfacing from sticking to your ironing surface.

Apply the Felted Wool Circles

1. Center a felted wool circle over a ring opening.

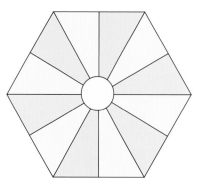

2. Stitch the felted wool circle to the ring using a decorative or straight stitch. Repeat for the 6 remaining wool circles.

Finishing

Layer the top, batting, and backing. Quilt and bind in the desired manner.

Gettin' Ziggy with It

Finished table runner: 17½˝ × 49½˝

These zigzag blocks are easier than they look. I can see this runner in so many different color and fabric combinations. It can be personalized for the seasons as well as a color scheme.

MATERIALS

Green: ⅓ yard

Blue: ½ yard

Print: 1¼ yards

Binding: ⅜ yard

Backing: ⅞ yard

Batting: 21˝ × 53˝

4½˝ × 4½˝ square template

CUTTING

Green

• Cut 6 strips 1½˝ × width of fabric.

Blue

• Cut 6 strips 1½˝ × width of fabric.

• Cut 3 strips 2˝ × width of fabric; subcut 2 strips 2˝ × 40½˝ and 2 strips 2˝ × 11½˝.

Print

• Cut 3 strips 1½˝ × width of fabric.

• Cut 3 strips 3½˝ × length of fabric; subcut 2 strips 3½˝ × 43½˝ and 2 strips 3½˝ × 17½˝.

Binding

• Cut 4 strips 2½˝ × width of fabric.

Make the Strip Set Blocks

1. Stitch together 2 blue strips, 2 green strips, and 1 print strip 1½˝ × width of fabric in the order shown. Make 3 strip sets. Press the seams in the direction of the arrow.

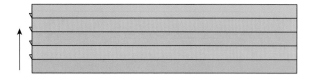

2. Lay 2 strip sets out so that one is facing right side up and one is facing wrong side up, with the print fabric at the top.

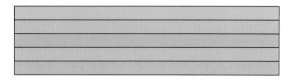

3. Measure the third strip set and find the center. Cut along the center.

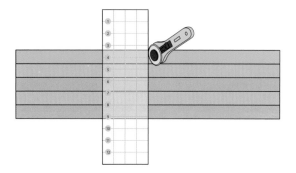

4. Lay one of the halves of the third strip set right side up and one wrong side up, with the print fabric at the top.

5. Place the 4½˝ square template on the strip set that is facing right side up. Align the template so that the upper left corner is touching the top of the strip set, the upper right corner is touching the seam between the print and the green strip, and the lower right corner is touching the bottom of the strip set.

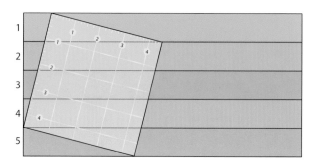

6. The template should be as far to the left end of the strip as possible so that all the required squares can be cut from the strip set.

7. Cut around the template.

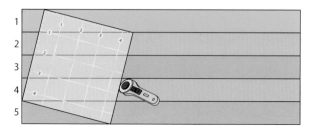

8. Repeat Steps 5–7 to cut a second square, placing the template next to the first cut and conserving as much of the fabric as possible. Using both of the strip sets that are right side up, cut a total of 10 squares 4½˝ × 4½˝.

9. Place the 4½˝ square template on a strip set that is facing wrong side up.

10. Repeat Steps 5–8 to cut a total of 10 squares 4½˝ × 4½˝ that are wrong side up.

Pair the Blocks

1. Turn all the blocks right side up.

2. Arrange a block together with a mirror-image block.

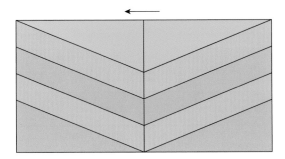

3. Stitch together. Open out and press the seam allowance to one side.

4. Sew 9 more pairs of blocks, 10 total.

5. Press the seam allowances for each pair in alternating directions so that the seam allowances will nest.

6. Stitch each pair together with another pair in a mirror image of each other, right sides together, along the edge with the print fabric. Use 2 pairs that have the seam allowances going in opposite directions. Refer to the photo (page 53) for placement.

Tip To make the seam allowances nest, stitch blocks together that have seam allowances going in different directions. That way they butt up against each other and your points will match!

7. Using the photo (page 53) as a reference, stitch all the blocks together.

8. Press the seam allowances to one side.

Add the Border

1. Stitch a 2″ × 40½″ blue strip to both long edges of the runner. Press the seam allowances toward the blue strips.

2. Stitch a 2″ × 11½″ blue strip to each end of the runner. Press the seam allowances toward the blue strips.

3. Sew a 3½″ × 43½″ print strip to each long edge of the runner. Press the seam allowances toward the print strips.

4. Sew a 3½″ × 17½″ print strip to the short ends of the runner. Press the seam allowances toward the print strips.

Finishing

Layer the top, batting, and backing. Quilt and bind in the desired manner.

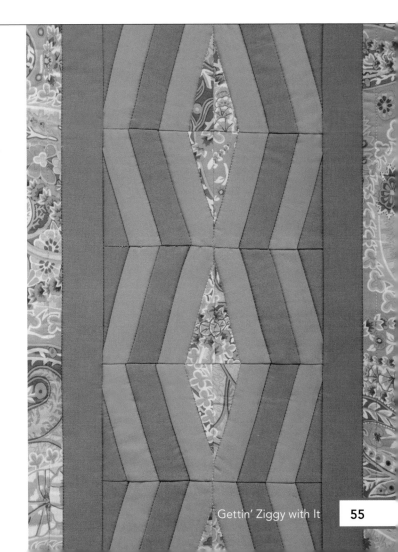

Have a Happy

Finished table runner: 20½″ × 50½″

The thing about most table runners, I think, is that they should be used for more than one occasion. This table runner would be equally at home for a birthday as it would for any celebration. The candles could also be made to look like sparklers! The fact that there is a large focus fabric makes it very adaptable.

MATERIALS

White solid: 1½ yards

Large-print focus fabric: ½ yard

Yellow solid: 1 fat eighth (9″ × 22″)

Polka dot prints: Scraps of multiple colors, enough to yield 24 strips 1″ × 5″

Orange jumbo rickrack: 2 yards

Pink jumbo rickrack: 2 yards

Binding: ⅓ yard   **Batting:** 24″ × 54″

Backing: 1 yard   **5½″ × 5½″ square template**

CUTTING

White solid

- Cut 6 strips 7½″ × width of fabric; subcut 48 rectangles 7½″ × 4½″.

- Cut 1 strip 2″ × width of fabric; subcut 24 rectangles 2″ × 1″.

Large-print focus fabric

- Cut 3 strips 4½″ × width of fabric; subcut 5 rectangles 4½″ × 22″.

Yellow solid

- Cut 2 strips 1″ × 22″.

Polka dot prints

- Cut 24 strips 1″ × 5″.

Orange jumbo rickrack

- Cut 3 pieces 22″ long.

Pink jumbo rickrack

- Cut 3 pieces 22″ long.

Binding

- Cut 4 strips 2½″ × width of fabric.

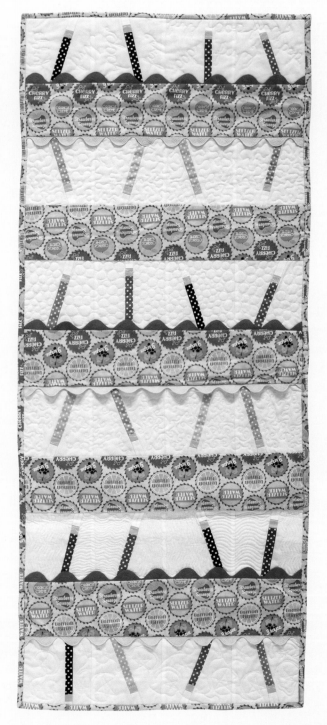

Make the Candle Blocks

1. Stitch 12 polka dot strips right sides together on a 1″ × 22″ yellow strip, sewing across the top of the polka dot strips.

2. Repeat Step 1 with the remaining polka dot strips and yellow strip.

3. Without pressing open, cut the yellow strip along the edges of the polka dot strips.

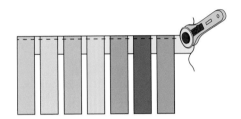

4. Press the yellow and polka dot strips open, pressing the seam allowances toward the yellow.

5. Stitch a 2″ × 1″ white rectangle to the yellow end of the polka dot / yellow unit. Open out and press the seam allowance toward the yellow. Repeat to make 24 candle units.

6. Stitch a candle unit to a 7½″ × 4½″ white rectangle along the 7½″ side of the rectangle, right sides together. Press the seam allowance toward the candle.

7. Sew a second 7½″ × 4½″ white rectangle on the opposite side of the candle. Press the seam allowance toward the candle.

8. Repeat Steps 6 and 7 to make 24 Candle blocks total.

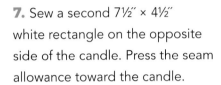
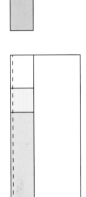

Cut the Candle Blocks

NOTE • The Candle blocks achieve their crooked or wonky look because the template with which they are cut is angled in different directions for trimming.

1. Lay a 5½″ × 5½″ square template over a Candle block. Tilt the template so that it is angled on the block.

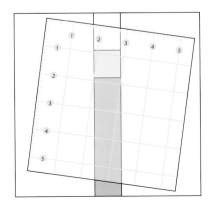

2. Cut around the template with a rotary cutter. The Candle block will now measure 5½″ × 5½″ square.

Tip Be cautious when handling the block after cutting it with the template. The edges are now on the bias. You may want to spray a little spray starch on it to keep it from stretching.

3. Repeat Steps 1 and 2 for all 24 Candle blocks, varying the placement and the angle at which the template is set on the blocks. Use the photo (previous page) for reference.

4. Stitch 4 Candle blocks together. Pin well, as the edges are slightly on the bias.

5. Open out and press the seam allowances to the side.

6. Repeat Steps 4 and 5 to make 6 rows of 4 Candle blocks each.

NOTE • The seam allowances on this table runner do not intersect with any other seam allowances, so it doesn't matter if they are pressed in any particular direction—just as long as they are pressed so they lie flat.

Assemble the Runner

NOTE • The width of the runner is 20½˝, but the focus-fabric rectangles are cut slightly longer. This is because the rickrack causes the fabric to "shrink" when it is sewn on (see Using Rickrack, page 9). The rectangles are trimmed to the correct length once the rickrack is sewn on.

1. Following the directions in Using Rickrack (page 9), baste the strips of rickrack to both long sides of 3 of the print strips.

2. Square the strips to 20½˝ long.

3. With right sides together, stitch a strip with rickrack to a Candle block row along the bottom edge of the candles—the edge where there is no yellow flame. Use a ¼˝ seam.

The edge of the rickrack should extend beyond the fabric.

4. Press the seam allowance toward the large-print strip.

5. On the opposite side of the same large-print strip, stitch another row of Candle blocks along the edge where there is no yellow flame.

6. Press the seam allowance toward the large-print strip.

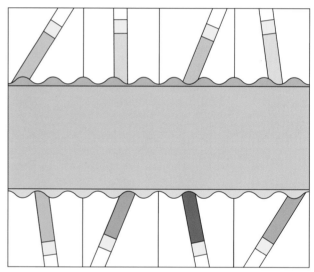

The rickrack edge should always be at the base of the candles.

7. With right sides together, add a large-print strip without rickrack to the Candle block strip on the flame side.

8. Press the seam toward the large-print strip.

9. Continue in this manner, adding the large-print strips to the candle strips, making certain that the flame edge is always along a large-print strip without rickrack. Use the photo (page 56) for reference.

10. Sew together all 6 Candle block strips and all 5 large-print strips.

Finishing

Layer the top, batting, and backing. Quilt and bind in the desired manner.

The Textured Table

Finished table runner: 14½″ × 50″

This runner is perfect for adding texture to your tabletop—sometimes you need something that adds a little more depth to your tablescape! This would be perfect for a fall dinner of venison or for a holiday celebration. Top it off with some antlers or wildlife-themed candlesticks!

NOTE • The seam allowance for luxe cuddle fabrics is ½″ as opposed to ¼″, so use ½″ seam allowances for all seams in this runner. Do not iron luxe cuddle fabric.

MATERIALS

Fox luxe cuddle: ¼ yard

Arctic lynx luxe cuddle: ¼ yard

Brown silk dupioni: 1 fat quarter (18″ × 22″)

Canvas metallic print: 1 fat quarter (18″ × 22″)

Brown cotton print: 1 fat quarter (18″ × 22″)

Dark metallic cotton print: 1 fat quarter (18″ × 22″) for leaves

Medium metallic cotton print: 1 fat quarter (18″ × 22″) for leaves

Light metallic cotton print: 1 fat quarter (18″ × 22″) for leaves

Binding: ⅓ yard

Backing: 1 yard

Batting: 20″ × 60″

CUTTING

Make a leaf template using The Textured Table leaf pattern (page 62).

Fox luxe cuddle

- Cut 3 strips 5½″ × 14½″.

Arctic lynx luxe cuddle

- Cut 3 strips 4½″ × 14½″.

Brown silk dupioni

- Cut 1 strip 5″ × 14½″.

Canvas metallic print

- Cut 2 strips 5½″ × 14½″.

Brown cotton print

- Cut 2 strips 4½″ × 14½″.

Dark metallic cotton print

- Cut 9 leaves.

Medium metallic cotton print

- Cut 14 leaves.

Light metallic cotton print

- Cut 13 leaves.

Binding

- Cut 4 strips 2½″ × width of fabric.

Make the Backing

1. Piece a 20″ × 60″ rectangle of backing fabric. Lay the backing rectangle wrong side up.

2. Place the batting on top of the wrong side of the backing.

3. Find and mark the centerline of the layered batting.

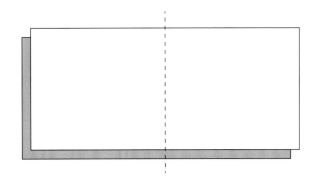

Add the Strips

1. Using the line that was marked for the center, lay a fox luxe cuddle strip so that the approximate center of the cuddle strip is laying over the center marking on the batting, right side up. Pin the strip or hand baste very securely through all layers.

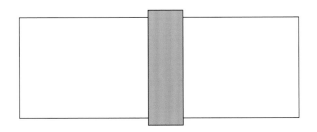

2. Lay a lynx luxe cuddle strip right sides together with the fox luxe cuddle strip. Pin very securely or hand baste along the long edge.

3. Stitch along the edge of the strips through all layers, using a ½″ seam allowance.

NOTE • It is very helpful when sewing with multiple thicker layers to use a walking foot and longer stitch length. If your normal stitch length is 2.5, increase your stitch length to 3.5.

4. Open the lynx luxe cuddle strip out. Smooth it outward with your hand, making certain that there are no creases or lumps in any of the layers.

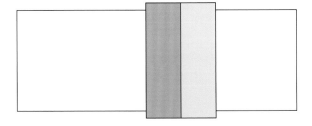

5. Hand baste or pin the lynx luxe cuddle strip through all layers.

6. Lay the silk dupioni strip right sides together with the fox luxe cuddle strip.

7. Pin or hand baste to the edge opposite the lynx luxe cuddle strip.

8. Stitch through all layers.

9. Open out the silk dupioni strip and smooth outward with your hand. Hand baste or pin very securely through all layers.

10. Repeat the assembly process using the remaining strips in the order shown in the photo (page 59) and the illustration.

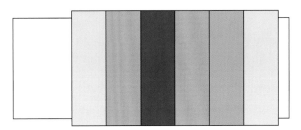

Add the Leaves

1. The leaves are added in a layered manner. On a brown print strip, measure and mark 1″ from the outside edges. Do not add leaves outside the 1″ marks.

2. Pleat a medium metallic leaf by pinching and creasing the center of the leaf about ½″ up from the base.

3. Lay the creased leaf near the center of the brown print strip and sew a ½″ seam from the base of the leaf up across the crease, creating a pleat. Sew through all layers.

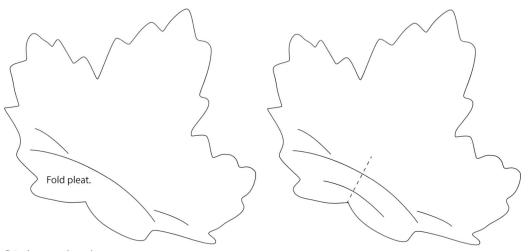

Fold pleat.

Stitch over the pleat.

4. Repeat Steps 2 and 3 to add 18 leaves total to the brown print strip. Alternate the leaves according to light, medium, and dark intensities.

5. Repeat Steps 1–4 for the other brown print strip.

Finishing

Trim and square up the runner, being cautious not to cut across any of the leaves. Bind the runner in your favorite manner.

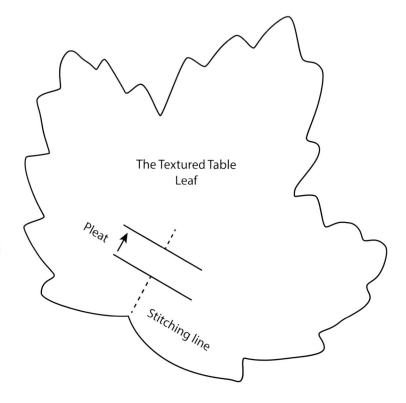

The Textured Table Leaf

Pleat

Stitching line

If I Knew You Were Coming

Finished table runner: 18½″ × 65½″

This is another large runner. A lot of people have large dining room tables or large farmhouse-style tables that dwarf a small table runner. This runner is a respectable size for a bigger tabletop. It would also be nice on top of an island in a kitchen. Since it isn't specific to a birthday celebration, it can be used for any type of party where cake is served. Remember: A party without a cake is just a meeting!

MATERIALS

Brown, teal, yellow, and pink: ¼ yard *each*

Cream: 1¾ yards

Print: ⅜ yard

Binding: ½ yard

Backing: 2 yards

Batting: 22″ × 69″

Jumbo rickrack: ¼ yard *each* of yellow, cream, pink, and brown

Woven fusible interfacing: 20″ wide, 1¼ yards

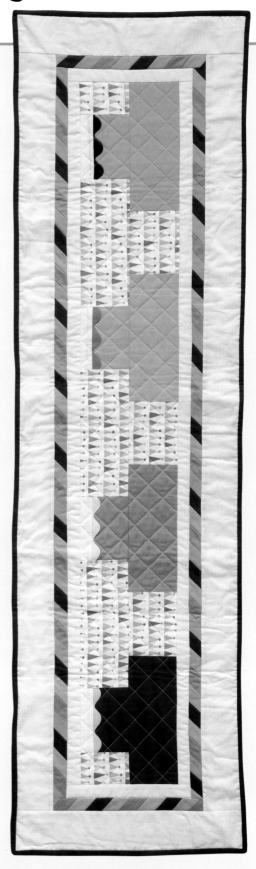

CUTTING

Brown, teal, yellow, and pink

From each color:

- Cut 1 strip 4½″ × width of fabric; subcut 1 rectangle 4½″ × 10½″ and 1 rectangle 3½″ × 5½″.

- Cut 2 strips 1½″ × width of fabric.

Cream

NOTE • The long border strips are cut along the length of the fabric as opposed to the width. Longer strips are needed so that they don't have to be pieced. These should be cut first so that there is enough fabric. The remaining pieces will be referred to as "width of fabric" but will be cut using the remaining width after the border pieces are cut.

- Cut 2 strips 3½″ × 59½″.

- Cut 2 strips 1½″ × 55½″.

- Cut 2 strips 3½″ × width of fabric; subcut 2 strips 3½″ × 18½″.

- Cut 2 strips 1½″ × width of fabric; subcut 2 strips 1½″ × 10½″ and 4 strips 1½″ × 5½″.

Print

- Cut 1 strip 4½″ × width of fabric; subcut 3 rectangles 4½″ × 5½″.

- Cut 1 strip 3½″ × width of fabric; subcut 3 rectangles 3½″ × 10½″ and 2 rectangles 3½″ × 3″.

Binding

- Cut 5 strips 2½″ × width of fabric.

Make the Striped Bias Border Strips

1. Arrange the 1½″ strips in the following order: brown, pink, teal, and yellow. Stitch together along the long edges. Press all seam allowances in one direction.

2. Repeat Step 1 and then sew both strip sets together, keeping the same color order. Press the seam allowance in the same direction as the other seam allowances.

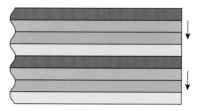

3. Cut a piece of the interfacing just slightly larger than the unit created in Step 2. Fuse it to the back, following the manufacturer's directions.

4. Lay a rotary-cutting ruler on the strip unit, aligning the 45° line with the bottom of the unit.

5. Make certain that you are not wasting any fabric by keeping the ruler as far to one side of the unit as possible but still covering all the strips.

6. Cut along the ruler to yield a bias edge.

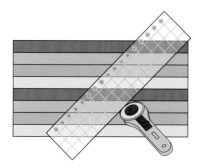

7. Move the ruler, placing the 1½″ line along the newly cut edge and including all the strips of fabric.

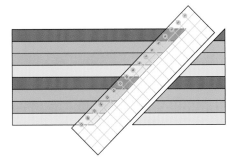

8. Cut a 1½″ strip.

9. Continue to cut along the edge until you have 14 striped bias strips.

10. Stitch the bias strips together until there are 2 continuous striped border strips 60″ long and 2 continuous striped border strips 14″ long.

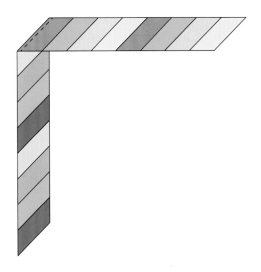

Make the Runner Center

1. Sew the cake bottom strip, alternating brown, teal, yellow, and pink rectangles 4½″ × 10½″ and 3 print rectangles 4½″ × 5½″. Press the seam allowances toward the solid rectangles.

2. Center the strip of yellow jumbo rickrack on the right side of the 3½″ × 5½″ brown rectangle so that the downward curves are centered across the rectangle. Use the photo (page 63) for reference.

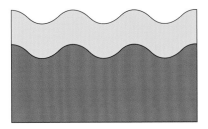

3. Referring to Using Rickrack (page 9), stitch the rickrack to the rectangle.

4. Repeat Steps 2 and 3 to add the cream rickrack to the teal rectangle, the pink rickrack to the yellow rectangle, and the brown rickrack to the pink rectangle.

5. Stitch a 1½″ × 5½″ cream rectangle to the rickrack side of each of the 4 rectangles from Steps 3 and 4.

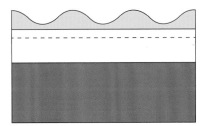

6. Trim the rickrack ends even with the rectangles.

7. Press the seam allowances toward the cream rectangles to complete the cake tops.

8. To make the cake-top strip, alternate stitching together 2 print rectangles 3½″ × 3″, 4 cake-top rectangles 3½″ × 5½″, and 3 print rectangles 3½″ × 10½″. Press the seam allowances toward the print rectangles.

9. With right sides together, stitch the cake-top strip to the cake-bottom strip, using the photo (page 63) for reference. Press the seam allowance toward the top strip.

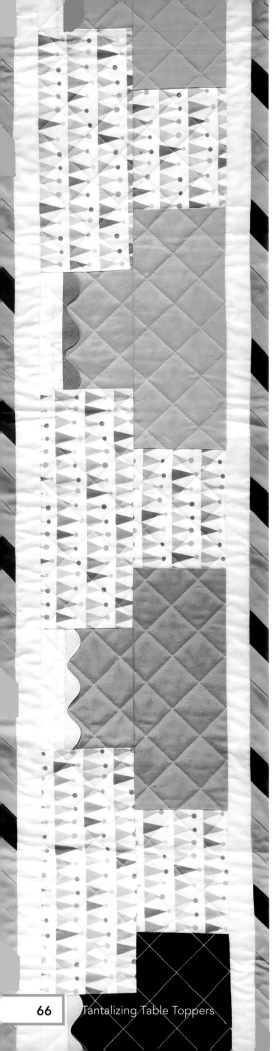

Add the Borders

1. Sew cream strips 1½″ × 55½″ to the top and bottom long edges of the cake section of the runner. Press the seam allowances toward the cake section of the runner.

2. Sew cream strips 1½″ × 10½″ to the short sides of the cake section of the table runner. Press.

NOTE • The stripe borders are sewn to the cream borders and then trimmed after sewing. Because there is interfacing on the back of them, it should prevent stretching. But care must be given to not stretch these and to prevent wavy borders.

3. Stitch the 2 striped 60″ bias strips to the top and bottom long edges of the runner; trim even. Press the seam allowances toward the striped bias border.

4. Stitch the 2 striped 14″ bias strips to the short sides of the runner; trim even. Press the seam allowances toward the striped bias border.

5. Sew the cream strips 3½″ × 59½″ to the long edges of the runner. Press the seam allowances toward the center.

6. Sew the cream strips 3½″ × 18½″ to the short edges of the runner. Press the seam allowances toward the center.

Finishing

Layer the top, batting, and backing. Quilt and bind in the desired manner.

The Fabric Makes It

Finished table runner: 14½″ × 38½″

This runner was designed with a very simple geometric because I wanted to use a textured fabric. The fabric makes the impact! If you are using a fabric that stands out as exceptional, you are going to need a simple design to showcase that fabric. Whether the fabric is textured or just a special print that you want to stand out, this is a great option.

MATERIALS

Rose, peach, and mint ruffled fabric:
⅛ yard *each*

Stone ruffled fabric: ¼ yard

Cream ruffled fabric: ⅜ yard

Binding: ⅓ yard

Backing: ½ yard

Batting: 18″ × 42″

CUTTING

Rose, peach, and mint ruffled fabric

From each color:

- Cut 1 strip 2½″ × width of fabric; subcut 2 rectangles 2½″ × 8½″ and 2 rectangles 2½″ × 4½″.

Stone ruffled fabric

- Cut 2 strips 2½″ × width of fabric; subcut 4 rectangles 2½″ × 8½″ and 4 rectangles 2½″ × 4½″.

Cream ruffled fabric

- Cut 3 strips 3½″ × width of fabric; subcut 2 rectangles 3½″ × 38½″, 2 rectangles 3½″ × 8½″, and 2 rectangles 2½″ × 4½″.

Binding

- Cut 3 strips 2½″ × width of fabric.

Make the Runner Center

1. Sew together a 2½˝ × 8½˝ stone rectangle, 2½˝ × 4½˝ rose rectangle, 2½˝ × 8½˝ mint rectangle, 2½˝ × 4½˝ peach rectangle, and 2½˝ × 8½˝ stone rectangle to make an outer row. Press the seam allowances open. Make 2.

2. Sew together a 2½˝ × 4½˝ stone rectangle, 2½˝ × 8½˝ rose rectangle, 2½˝ × 4½˝ mint rectangle, 2½˝ × 8½˝ peach rectangle, and 2½˝ × 4½˝ stone rectangle to make a center row. Press the seam allowances open. Make 2.

3. Stitch the center rows together on a long edge; press the seam open. Add a 2½˝ × 4½˝ cream rectangle to each end. Press the seams open.

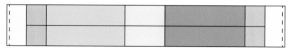

4. Sew the outer rows to the center section to complete the runner center. Press the seams open.

Add the Border

1. Stitch the 3½˝ × 8½˝ cream rectangles to the short edges of the runner. Press the seams open.

2. Stitch the 3½˝ × 38½˝ cream rectangles to the long edges of the runner. Press the seams open.

Finishing

Layer the top, batting, and backing. Quilt and bind in the desired manner.

Catch of the Day

Finished table runner: 16½″ × 53½″

In Wisconsin we have this lovely tradition of having fish fries on Friday nights. Usually a cocktail called a Brandy Old-Fashioned Sweet accompanies these. Most of the time we go out to a pub or restaurant, but wouldn't it be fun to do a fish supper at home for friends and decorate with this table runner? Another idea for this runner: Throw a mermaid party!

Before we can discuss how to put this runner together, we need to talk about sewing curves. This runner is all curves. They aren't as hard as you might think, so don't let it scare you off.

MATERIALS

Assorted turquoise and green prints: 1 fat eighth (9″ × 22″) each of 22 prints

Red: 1 square 5″ × 5″

Light print: ⅓ yard

Woven fusible interfacing: 20″ wide, ¼ yard

Binding: ⅜ yard

Backing: 1 yard

Batting: 20″ × 57″

CUTTING

Make a clamshell template with the Catch of the Day clamshell pattern (page 74).

Assorted turquoise and green prints

- Cut a total of 111 clamshells.

Red

- Cut 1 clamshell.

Light print

- Cut 1 rectangle 9½″ × 16½″.

Woven fusible interfacing

- Cut 1 rectangle 5½″ × 16½″.

Binding

- Cut 4 strips 2½″ × width of fabric.

Sew the Curves

This quilt is basically a one-patch. There is no piecing within the individual clamshells, so it goes together rather quickly once you get in the piecing groove.

Each piece looks as shown (at right). The side of the curve that goes outward is *convex*, and the side that goes inward is *concave*. Always sew with the concave on the underside and the convex on top; this prevents stretching. The concave side stretches more than the convex, so it's good to have it against the sewing machine feed dogs.

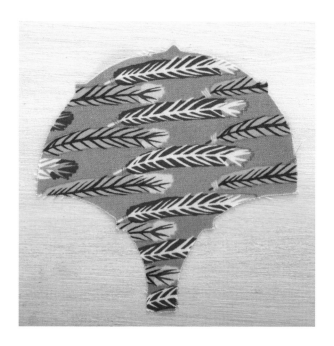

1. When you sew 2 clamshells together, work from left to right. Place the clamshells as shown, with the points north and the curve south, right sides up.

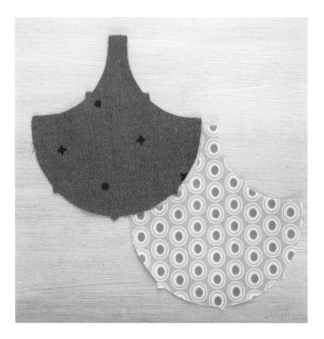

2. Place the left clamshell wrong side up, with the centerline at the beginning of the right clamshell's concave curve and the "stem" of the left clamshell now south.

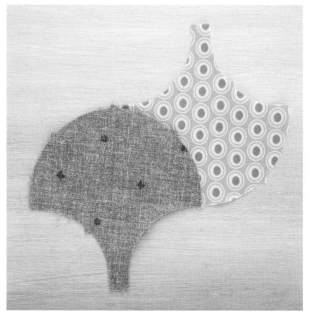

NOTE • These clamshells were cut using a die-cutter, but these can be cut using the Catch of the Day pattern (page 74).

The clamshells are right sides together. The convex side will be sewn to the concave side of the clamshell that is lying right side up. When the clamshells are sewn together, you are actually simultaneously working on the first 2 rows.

3. Hold the top clamshell up at an almost vertical angle as you sew the edges together. Always use the needle-down feature on your sewing machine, or manually stop with the needle down.

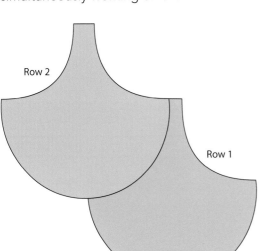

4. Continue to hold the top clamshell up vertically as you sew the edges together using a ¼˝ seam allowance. You can always lift your presser foot up and adjust, as long as you are stopping with the needle down and in the fabric.

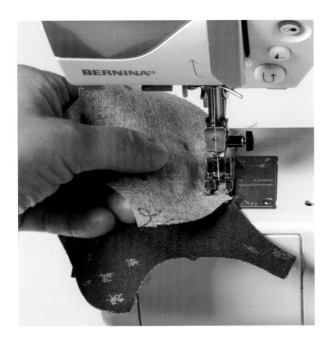

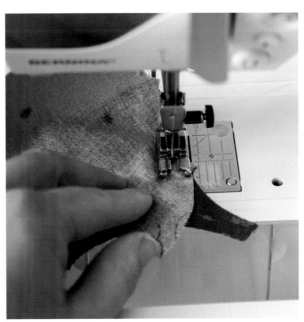

5. Stop stitching ¼˝ from the end. Do not backstitch. Press the seam allowance toward the convex curve.

6. Sew the next clamshell by using the same setup. Choose the next clamshell and place it with the stem south and the curve north.

7. Bring the unsewn clamshell down so that the stem is facing north with the right side up; then overlap the other 2 sewn clamshells wrong side up.

8. Sew the curve by putting the convex curve on top along the right side of the new clamshell.

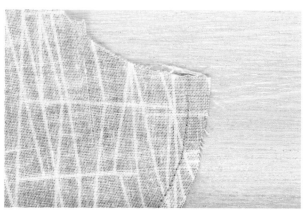

Start ¼˝ in from the edge.

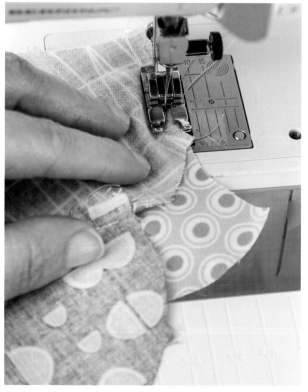

Tantalizing Table Toppers

9. Press the seam allowance toward the convex curve.

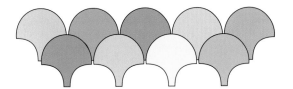

10. Repeat Steps 1–9 until you have 5 on top and 4 below. Every other row will have 5 clamshells, and alternate rows will have 4.

11. Refer to the photo (page 69) to help place the clamshells. Continue adding rows until you have used all 112 clamshells.

Sew the Interfacing

1. Place the 5½″ × 16½″ interfacing rectangle fusible side up. Place the scalloped end of the runner right side down onto the interfacing.

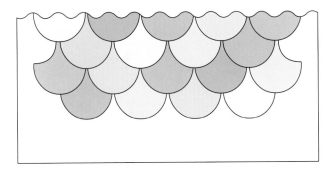

2. Stitch along the curved edges using an ⅛″ seam allowance. Make certain to stitch all the way to the clamshells in the next row. Pivot as you come to the clamshell in the next row; then sew along the next curve.

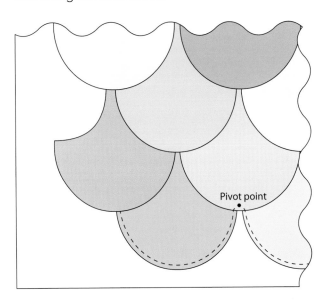

Pivot point

3. Make certain to keep the edges of the clamshells free when pivoting.

4. Sew all the curved edges to the end.

5. Clip the pivot points.

6. Turn the fusible toward the wrong side of the runner, making certain to smooth the rounded edges of the clamshells.

Tip It helps to use a turning bodkin for this purpose. It will help you get those curves out and smooth.

7. Lay the fusible side of the runner over the right side of the print rectangle so that the scallops are over half of the print rectangle.

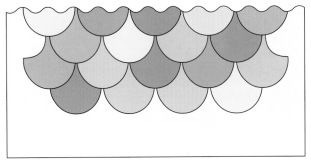

8. Press with a hot iron through all layers so that the fusible sticks to the print rectangle. Edgestitch the scalloped edge.

9. Trim the long edges of the runner even, ¼″ outside the shorter rows.

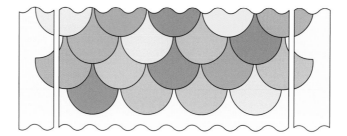

10. Trim the short, concave end of the runner even with the "stems" of the second row of clamshells.

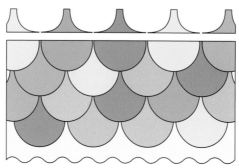

Finishing

Layer the top, batting, and backing. Quilt and bind in the desired manner.

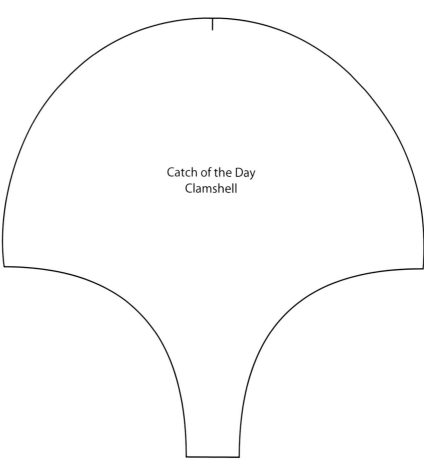

Catch of the Day
Clamshell

Panel Discussion

Finished table runner: 15½″ × 60½″

Over the last few years, some of the best fabric designers have created panels that are just stunning. One of the problems with panels is that they tend to stifle creativity. It's very hard when you're looking at one to think of anything other than block after block; that's because they are arranged like that on the bolt of fabric.

Let's look at panels from a different perspective. Should they challenge creativity? I have seen quilts where people have sliced up part of a panel and added other fabric. That's interesting! Why couldn't you cut a panel up and use certain sections? You wouldn't have to necessarily center the main image. Sometimes images are best when only a part of them are showing.

With this runner, I took apart a panel by one of my favorite artists. I added triangles in the corners and offset the panel squares, which measure 7½″ before being stitched in. You could use this pattern and cut 7½″ squares from any panel or try it in different sizes.

The main idea here is that whatever the panel patch size, you add strips around it until it equals 12½″. For example, if your patch size were 5½″, then your strips around the block on either side would then have to total 7″ when stitched in. The cut width of the strips may be 6½″ and 1½″. Or they may be 4½″ and 3½″. See what you think!

MATERIALS

Fabric panel with at least 5 images

Print: ⅞ yard

Assorted scraps of 11 different fabrics, each large enough to yield 4½″ × 4½″ squares

Binding: ⅜ yard

Backing: 1 yard

Batting: 19″ × 64″

CUTTING

Fabric panel

- Cut 5 panel squares 7½˝ × 7½˝.

Print

- Cut 1 strip 4½˝ × width of fabric; subcut 3 rectangles 4½˝ × 12½˝, 1 rectangle 4½˝ × 9½˝, and 1 rectangle 4½˝ × 8½˝.

- Cut 3 strips 3½˝ × width of fabric; subcut 1 rectangle 3½˝ × 30½˝, 1 rectangle 3½˝ × 21½˝, 1 rectangle 3½˝ × 12½˝, 1 rectangle 3½˝ × 10½˝, 1 rectangle 3½˝ × 9½˝, 1 rectangle 3½˝ × 8½˝, and 2 rectangles 3½˝ × 7½˝.

- Cut 2 strips 2½˝ × width of fabric; subcut 1 rectangle 2½˝ × 12½˝, 1 rectangle 2½˝ × 10½˝, 1 rectangle 2½˝ × 8½˝, and 2 rectangles 2½˝ × 7½˝.

- Cut 2 strips 1½˝ × width of fabric; subcut 1 rectangle 1½˝ × 12½˝, 1 rectangle 1½˝ × 9½˝, 1 rectangle 1½˝ × 8½˝, and 2 rectangles 1½˝ × 7½˝.

Assorted scraps

- Cut 4 squares 4½˝ × 4½˝, 6 squares 3½˝ × 3½˝, and 1 square 2½˝ × 2½˝.

Binding

- Cut 4 strips 2½˝ × width of fabric.

Make the Blocks

NOTE • All seam allowances are pressed toward the strips after each strip is sewn on. There is no matching of seams in this runner.

BLOCK 1

1. Stitch a 3½˝ × 7½˝ print rectangle to the right side of one of the panel squares.

2. Stitch a 3½˝ × 10½˝ print rectangle to the top of the unit.

3. Stitch a 2½˝ × 10½˝ print rectangle to the left side of the unit.

4. Stitch a 2½˝ × 12½˝ print rectangle to the bottom of the unit.

5. Lay a 4½˝ × 4½˝ assorted square on the lower right corner of the block, right sides together.

6. Draw a diagonal line from the upper right corner to the lower left corner of the square.

7. Stitch just to the outside of the line.

8. Trim the underside of the assorted square between the top half and the print fabric.

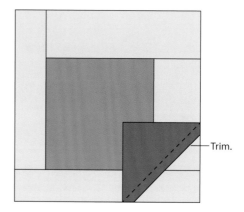

9. Fold the triangle over the corner of the block and press.

BLOCK 2

1. Lay a 4½″ × 4½″ assorted square on the lower right corner of one of the panel squares.

2. Repeat Block 1, Steps 6–9 (previous page).

3. Stitch a 1½″ × 7½″ print rectangle to the top of the panel square.

4. Stitch a 3½″ × 8½″ print rectangle to the right side of the unit.

5. Stitch a 2½″ × 8½″ print rectangle to the left side of the unit.

6. Stitch a 4½″ × 12½″ print rectangle to the bottom of the unit.

7. Lay a 3½″ × 3½″ assorted square on the lower left corner of the block.

8. Repeat Block 1, Steps 6–9 (previous page), except draw the line on the square from the upper left corner to the lower right corner.

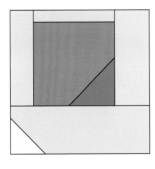

BLOCK 3

1. Lay a 3½″ × 3½″ assorted square on the lower right corner of a panel square.

2. Follow Block 1, Steps 6–9 (previous page) to add the assorted square to the corner.

3. Stitch a 1½″ × 7½″ print rectangle to the top of the unit.

4. Stitch a 1½″ × 8½″ print rectangle to the right side of the unit.

5. Stitch a 4½″ × 8½″ print rectangle to the bottom of the unit.

6. Stitch a 4½″ × 12½″ print rectangle to the left side of the unit.

7. Lay a 3½″ × 3½″ assorted square on the lower left corner of the block.

8. Repeat Block 1, Steps 6–9 (previous page), except draw the line on the square from the upper left corner to the lower right corner.

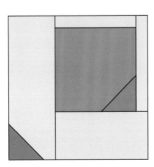

BLOCK 4

1. Lay a 2½″ × 2½″ assorted square on the lower left corner of a panel square.

2. Follow Block 1, Steps 6–9 (previous page) to add the square in the corner, except draw the line from the upper left corner of the square to the lower right corner.

3. Stitch a 2½″ × 7½″ print rectangle to the top of the unit.

4. Stitch a 3½″ × 7½″ print rectangle to the bottom of the unit.

5. Stitch a 1½″ × 12½″ print rectangle to the right side of the unit.

6. Stitch a 4½″ × 12½″ print rectangle to the left side of the unit.

7. Lay a 4½″ × 4½″ assorted square on the lower left corner of the block.

8. Follow Block 1, Steps 6–9 (previous page) to add the square to the block, except draw the line from the upper left corner to the lower right corner.

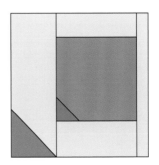

BLOCK 5

1. Lay a 4½″ × 4½″ assorted square on the lower right corner of a panel square.

2. Follow Block 1, Steps 6–9 (page 76) to add the square to the corner.

3. Stitch a 2½″ × 7½″ print rectangle to the top of the unit.

4. Stitch a 1½″ × 9½″ print rectangle to the left side of the unit.

5. Stitch a 4½″ × 9½″ print rectangle to the right side of the unit.

6. Stitch a 3½″ × 12½″ print rectangle to the bottom of the unit.

7. Lay a 3½″ × 3½″ assorted square on the lower right corner of the block.

8. Follow Block 1, Steps 6–9 (page 76) to add the square to the corner.

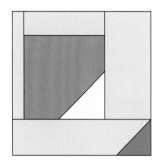

Add the Border Strip

NOTE • The border on this runner is only on one side to give it an asymmetrical look.

1. Lay a 3½″ × 3½″ assorted square on one end of the 3½″ × 21½″ print rectangle.

2. Follow Block 1, Steps 6–9 (page 76) to add the square to the rectangle.

3. Lay a 3½″ × 3½″ assorted square on one end of the 3½″ × 30½″ print rectangle.

4. Follow Block 1, Steps 6–9 (page 76) to add the square to the rectangle, except draw the line from the upper left corner to the lower right corner of the square.

5. Sew the rectangles together to make the border strip.

6. Stitch the border strip to the left side of the runner. Press the seam allowance toward the border strip.

Finishing

Layer the top, batting, and backing. Quilt and bind in the desired manner.

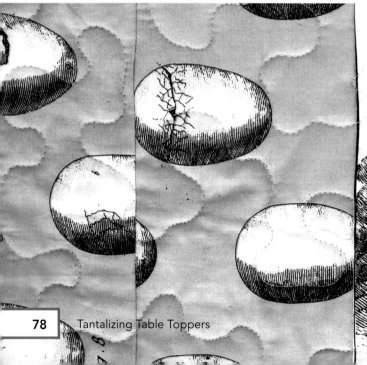

Place Mats and Napkins

These are items that are not likely to be used for napkin rings, and napkin rings can be edible!

I always encourage customers who come into my shop to indulge themselves by making items for their table. So often, people will find a piece of fabric that they are in love with, but they won't know what to use it for. At this time, I will often suggest that they buy enough to make some table napkins. Cloth napkins are a delight!

If you currently use paper napkins, you know what a waste they are. You wipe your mouth or face once with them, and they are all used up. With a cloth napkin, you will be able to use it throughout the meal, and you can look at that lovely fabric the entire time. What could be better? I have cloth napkins that have lasted for years. Make sure that you hang them dry, and you won't ever have to iron them.

Think about using unexpected items as napkin rings. Napkin rings add dimension to a table, and an unexpected surprise is always fun.

Simple Double-Sided Napkins

Finished napkin: 19½″ × 19½″

MATERIALS

NOTE • The materials are for 2 large dinner-size napkins. If you want to make more of these, multiply the materials by the quantity needed.

Green check: ⅝ yard

Red print: ⅝ yard

CUTTING

Green check and red print

From each fabric:

• Cut 2 squares 20″ × 20″.

Make the Napkins

1. Lay one red print square right sides together with a green check square.

2. Stitch ¼″ around the entire perimeter of the square, leaving a 4″ opening for turning right side out.

3. Turn right side out.

4. Press the napkin, making certain to push out the corners with a turning bodkin or wooden skewer.

Tip It is helpful to run the turning bodkin or wooden skewer around the inside perimeter of the napkin to make certain, as you press, that the seam is fully turned outward.

5. Turn the edges of the opening inward and press.

6. Topstitch around the entire perimeter of the napkin, making sure to stitch the opening closed.

7. Repeat Steps 1–6 to make the second napkin.

Arrange your napkins in a drinking glass or Mason jar to fit the theme of your table.

Canning Jar Place Mat

Finished place mat: 16½″ × 20½″

MATERIALS

NOTE • The pattern is for 1 place mat. Multiply the materials by the number of place mats you wish to make.

Red print: 1 fat quarter (18″ × 22″)

Gray print: ⅛ yard

White: ⅓ yard

Backing: 1 fat quarter (18″ × 22″)

Batting: 18″ × 22″

CUTTING

Red print

• Cut 1 rectangle 16½″ × 17½″.

Gray print

• Cut 1 rectangle 3½″ × 10½″.

White

• Cut 6 squares 3½″ × 3½″.

• Cut 2 strips 2½″ × width of fabric for the binding.

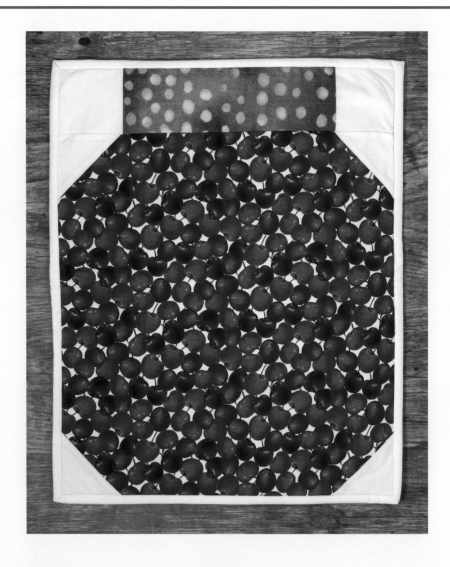

Make the Place Mat

1. Draw a diagonal line from corner to corner across 4 white squares.

2. Lay one white square on each of the 4 corners of the red print rectangle.

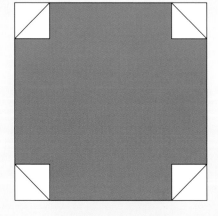

3. Stitch on the diagonal line of each of the white squares.

4. Trim the corners of the red print fabric and the white squares.

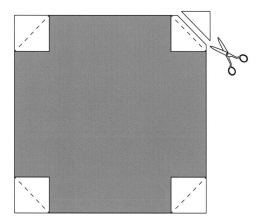

5. Press the remaining white triangles outward to complete the jar unit.

6. Join the 2 remaining white squares to the short sides of the gray rectangle. Press the seam allowances toward the gray rectangle. This is the lid unit.

7. Stitch the lid unit to the jar unit along the 16½″ side and press the seam allowance toward the red print.

8. Layer the place mat, the batting, and the backing. Add quilting if desired.

9. Trim the backing and batting even with the place mat.

10. Bind using the 2½″ white strips.

Mitered Hemmed Napkins

Finished napkin: 14″ × 14″

NOTE • The finished size of these may be slightly larger or smaller than 14″ × 14″, allowing for some variation in hem size by the maker. To get the edges well mitered, occasionally a difference of ⅛″ or so may occur.

Did you know that there are actually different size recommendations for different types of napkins? Well, luncheon napkins are generally smaller than dinner napkins. Clearly, a cocktail napkin is going to be much smaller. These napkins are luncheon sized, but you certainly could use this size as your everyday supper size. They will wash up beautifully year after year.

MATERIALS

NOTE • The quantity of fabric is for 2 luncheon-sized napkins. Multiply the amount of fabric by the number of napkins needed.

Aqua print: ½ yard

CUTTING

Aqua print

• Cut 2 squares 15″ × 15″.

Make the Napkins

1. Turn each corner of the square inward 1″ along a 45° line. Press.

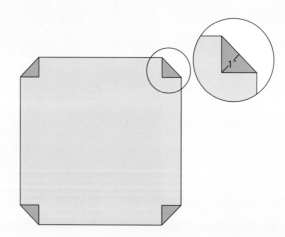

2. Trim the corners about ¼˝ from the folds.

3. Turn the edges of the square in around the entire perimeter of the square ¼˝ and press.

4. Turn the pressed edges in ¼˝ around the entire perimeter of the square, mitering the corners. Pin.

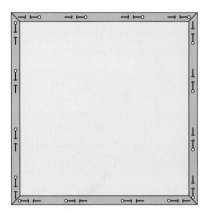

5. Stitch along the turned edge closest to the center of the napkin.

6. Repeat Steps 1–5 to make the second napkin.

Tip It is important to stay as close to this folded edge as possible without falling off the edge. This will keep all the edges from turning outward after years of laundering.

Mitered Hemmed Napkins   **85**

Scallop Place Mats

Finished place mat: 13½″ × 19½″

MATERIALS

NOTE • The amounts listed are for 2 place mats. Multiply the amounts by the number of place mats you need.

Orange print: ½ yard

Aqua print: ½ yard

White: ¼ yard

Woven interfacing: 20″ wide, ⅜ yard

Batting: 2 pieces each 15″ × 21″

CUTTING

Make a template with the Scallop Place Mat pattern (page 89).

Orange print

- Cut 2 rectangles 13½″ × 19½″. Trim the scallop end using the scallop place mat template.
- Cut 2 of scallop place mat for facing.

Aqua print

- Cut 2 rectangles 15½″ × 21½″.

White

- Cut 2 rectangles 6″ × 13½″.

Woven interfacing

- Cut 2 rectangles 6″ × 13½″.

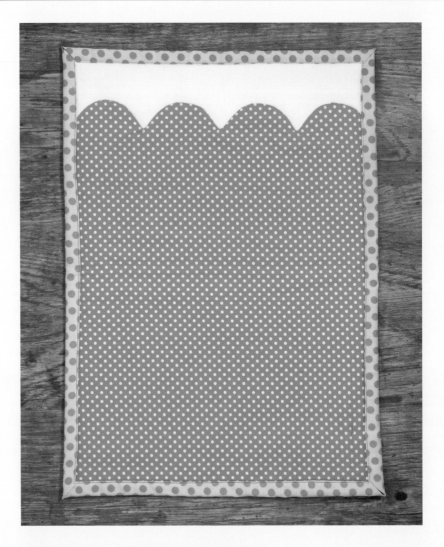

Make the Place Mats

1. Lay the scallop facing right sides together with the orange-print scallop piece.

2. Stitch a ⅛″ seam allowance around the edges of the scallop, starting at the dot and ending at the opposite dot.

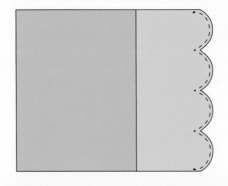

3. Clip the inner corners, using caution to not cut beyond the stitching line.

Tip You may want to reinforce the inner corners by stitching over them a second time so that there isn't a weakness created when you clip.

4. Turn the facing right side out using a turning bodkin or wooden skewer.

Tip When using a turning bodkin or a wooden skewer, be careful to push the seam out as far as it goes—but be gentle. Don't puncture your seam allowance.

5. Press the scalloped edge.

6. Fuse a woven interfacing rectangle to the wrong side of the white rectangle.

7. Lay the scalloped edge right side up over the white rectangle. The scallop should be laid over the white rectangle so that the entire length of the finished rectangle measures 19½˝. Pin.

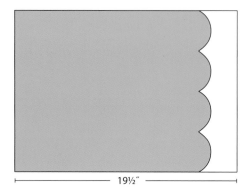

19½˝

8. Stitch the edge of the scallop onto the white fabric through all layers.

9. Layer the aqua rectangle wrong side up, the batting rectangle, and the finished scalloped unit right side up.

10. Trim the batting to the same size as the finished top unit.

11. Using a quilting ruler, trace the corners of the place mat onto the backing using a marking pen.

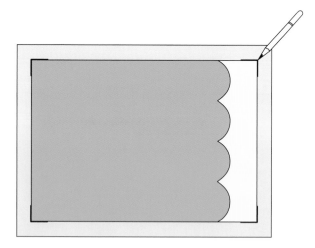

12. Using the 45° angle on a quilting ruler, draw a 45° line across each corner.

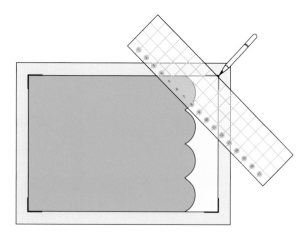

13. Remove the top layer and the batting; set aside.

14. Fold a corner right sides together, matching the 45° lines.

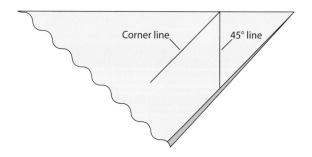

Corner line   45° line

15. Stitch from the inside corner, stopping ⅛″ from the edge. Trim ¼″ from the edge.

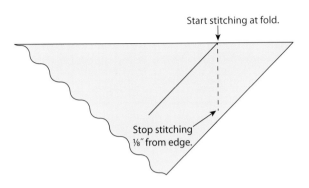

Start stitching at fold.

Stop stitching ⅛″ from edge.

16. Repeat Steps 14 and 15 for all 4 corners. Turn right side out.

17. Place the batting and place mat top back inside the backing, pushing it into the corners and the edges. Flatten and smooth.

18. Turn the edges of the aqua rectangle under ⅛″ and pin all around the perimeter.

19. Topstitch along the folded edge.

20. Repeat Steps 1–19 to make the second place mat.

Scallop Place Mat
Cut 2 for facing.

Place on fold.

Textured Place Mats

Finished place mat: 12½″ × 18½″

This set of place mats goes beautifully with The Textured Table (page 59). Using faux fur in a tablescape is nothing short of brilliant. This is especially beautiful during the winter, when hot soups and stews and lush faux hides make us feel warm and cozy. Faux fur is easily laundered. If you hang them to dry, they need no further care. However, they are not a friend of the iron.

MATERIALS

NOTE • The amounts listed are for 2 place mats. Multiply the amounts by the number of place mats you need.

Faux fur or plush fabric: ½ yard

Gold metallic fabric: ¼ yard

Backing: ½ yard

Batting: 2 pieces each 13″ × 19″

CUTTING

Faux fur or plush fabric

• Cut 2 rectangles 13″ × 14″.

Gold metallic fabric

• Cut 2 rectangles 5½″ × 13″.

Backing

• Cut 2 rectangles 13″ × 19″.

Make the Place Mats

1. With right sides together, stitch a gold metallic rectangle to a faux fur rectangle along the 13″ edge.

2. On the wrong side, use a pressing wheel or stick to press the seam allowance flat toward the plush fabric. This is the place mat unit.

3. Layer the backing rectangle with the place mat unit, right sides together.

4. Layer the batting against the wrong side of the place mat unit.

5. Pin all 3 layers securely. Hand baste if needed.

6. Using a walking foot and a longer stitch length, machine stitch around the entire perimeter of the place mat unit / backing / batting sandwich, leaving a 4˝ opening along a short edge of the plush fabric.

7. Turn right side out.

8. Using a turning bodkin or wooden skewer, gently push the seam allowances out.

9. Use a pressing wheel to flatten the edges.

10. Hand stitch the opening closed.

11. Apply quilting in your favorite manner to the gold rectangle section of the place mat.

12. Repeat Steps 1–11 to make the second place mat.

Cocktail Napkins

Finished napkin: 5½″ × 5½″

MATERIALS

NOTE • The amounts listed are for 4 napkins. Multiply the amounts by the number of napkins you need.

Pink print: 1 fat quarter (18″ × 22″)

Red diagonal stripe: 1 fat quarter (18″ × 22″)

Woven fusible interfacing: 20″ wide, ⅓ yard

CUTTING

Pink print
- Cut 4 squares 5½″ × 5½″.

Red diagonal stripe
- Cut 4 squares 7½″ × 7½″.

Woven fusible interfacing
- Cut 4 squares 5½″ × 5½″.

Make the Napkins

NOTE • You may find the need to cut about ⅛″ off all sides of the 5½″ pink print squares when inserting them inside the border fabric. It all depends on your choice of fabrics and how they behave once they are interfaced and pressed.

1. Fuse an interfacing square to the wrong side of each 5½″ × 5½″ pink print square.

2. Lay a 7½″ × 7½″ striped square wrong side up.

3. Center a fused pink print square on top of the striped square, right side up.

4. With a marking pen and ruler, trace the corners of the fused square. Set the fused square aside.

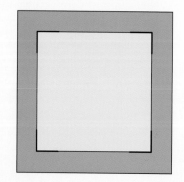

5. Using a ruler with a 45°-angle marking, align the 45°-angle line with the corner tracing.

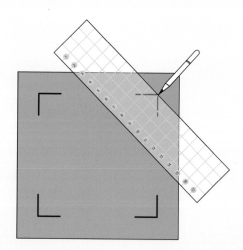

6. Draw a 45°-angle line on the 7½″ × 7½″ square on all 4 corners.

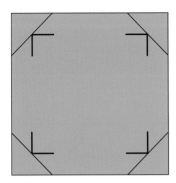

7. Fold a corner of the 7½″ × 7½″ square right sides together along the 45° line.

8. Stitch along the line that was drawn, starting at the folded corner and stopping ⅛″ away from the end.

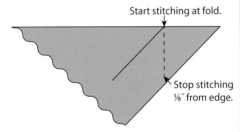

Start stitching at fold.

Stop stitching ⅛″ from edge.

9. Repeat for all 4 corners.

10. Trim the excess fabric beyond the stitching line at each corner.

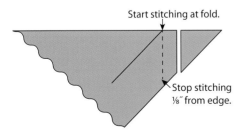

Start stitching at fold.

Stop stitching ⅛″ from edge.

11. Turn the corners right side out.

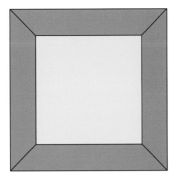

12. Place the fused square inside the mitered 7½″ × 7½″ square so that the mitered square borders it. Press.

13. Turn the raw edge of the mitered square under ⅛″ and stitch along the folded edge.

Tip It helps to use a wooden skewer to turn these edges under. It is similar to needle-turn appliqué, but you are stitching with your sewing machine.

14. Repeat Steps 2–13 to make the 3 remaining napkins.

Simple Linen Place Mats

Finished place mat: 15½˝ × 20½˝

There are so many beautiful printed linen fabrics on the market today. They're perfect for table settings.

MATERIALS

NOTE • The amounts listed are for 4 place mats. Multiply the amounts by the number of place mats you need.

Metallic small-dot linen: 1 yard

Metallic large-dot linen: ½ yard

Metallic black-deer linen print: ½ yard

Woven fusible interfacing: 20˝ wide, 2⅜ yards

CUTTING

Metallic small-dot linen

• Cut 4 rectangles 16˝ × 21˝.

Metallic large-dot linen

• Cut 2 rectangles 16˝ × 21˝.

Metallic black-deer linen print

• Cut 2 rectangles 16˝ × 21˝.

Woven fusible interfacing

• Cut 4 rectangles 16˝ × 21˝.

Make the Place Mats

1. Press the fusible interfacing rectangles to the wrong sides of the small-dot linen rectangles.

2. Place a small-dot linen rectangle and a large-dot or deer-print rectangle right sides together. Stitch a ¼˝ seam around the entire perimeter, leaving an opening for turning.

3. Turn right side out.

4. Using a turning bodkin or wooden skewer, gently push the seam allowances out. Press, turning the edges of the opening in.

5. Topstitch ⅛˝ around the outside edge, stitching the opening closed.

6. Repeat the topstitching 1˝ in from the first stitching.

7. Repeat Steps 2–6 for a total of 4 place mats.

About the Author

JUDY GAUTHIER is the owner of Bungalow Quilting & Yarn, a modern quilt shop in Ripon, Wisconsin. A mother, wife, and registered nurse, she is also a faculty member of Wisconsin Public Television and Nancy Zieman Productions' Quilt Expo and for International Quilt Festival. Judy has designed a fabric line for Ink & Arrow for QT Fabrics. She resides in Ripon, Wisconsin, with her husband of 33 years and their cockapoo, Rico. *Tantalizing Table Toppers* is Judy's fourth book with C&T Publishing.

Visit Judy online and follow on social media!

Website: bungalowquilting.com

Facebook: /bungalowquilting

Instagram: @bungalowquilting

Also by Judy Gauthier:

    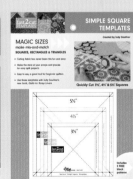

Want even more creative content?

Go to ctpub.com/offer

& sign up to receive our gift to you!

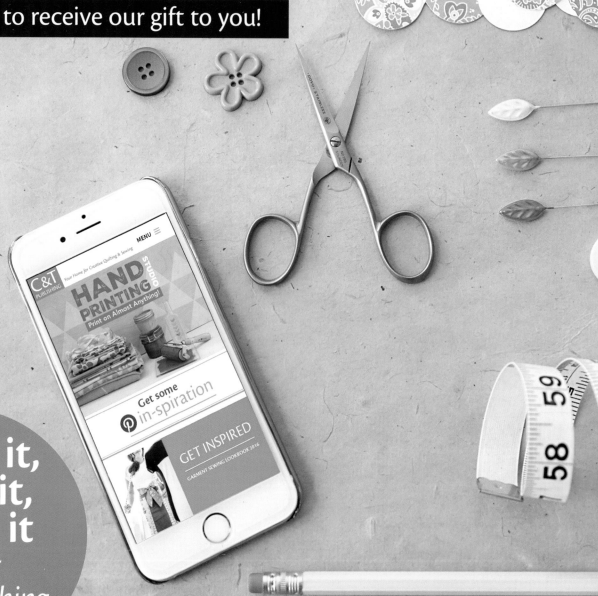

Make it, snap it, share it *using #ctpublishing*